Cults

Battle of the Angels

Journeys of Faith®
1-800-633-2484

Bob & Penny Lord

Other Books by Bob and Penny Lord

THIS IS MY BODY, THIS IS MY BLOOD
Miracles of the Eucharist - Book I
THIS IS MY BODY, THIS IS MY BLOOD
Miracles of the Eucharist - Book II
THE MANY FACES OF MARY
a Love Story
WE CAME BACK TO JESUS
SAINTS AND OTHER POWERFUL WOMEN
IN THE CHURCH
SAINTS AND OTHER POWERFUL MEN
IN THE CHURCH
HEAVENLY ARMY OF ANGELS
SCANDAL OF THE CROSS AND ITS TRIUMPH
MARTYRS - THEY DIED FOR CHRIST
THE ROSARY - THE LIFE OF JESUS AND MARY
VISIONARIES, MYSTICS AND STIGMATISTS
VISIONS OF HEAVEN, HELL & PURGATORY
ESTE ES MI CUERPO, ESTA ES MI SANGRE
Milagros de la Eucaristía
LOS MUCHOS ROSTROS DE MARIA
una historia de amor

Table of Contents

The Battle of the Angels
The Angels battle the Powers of Hell

My brothers and sisters, there is a battle raging. The enemy's plan is that the intended victims, those dead bodies which are to be strewn along the side of the road leading to Paradise, are to be you and me, our children and loved ones. We are waist-deep in war. Never has it been more obvious than in these, the last days of the Second Millennium. We have been warned throughout Scripture about the battle between the Angels and the devil, between Michael and his Heavenly Army of Angels against Satan and the fallen angels.

"Then a great war broke out in Heaven; Michael and his Angels battled against the dragon. The dragon and its angels fought back, but they did not prevail and there was no longer any place for them in Heaven."[1]

Now we have been told, you can't take the Book of Revelation too seriously. It's very symbolic. So we go to one of the most brilliant writers in the New Testament, St. Paul the Apostle. In Ephesians, he warns us:

"Put on the armor of God so that you may be able to stand firm against the wiles of the devil. For our struggle is not with flesh and blood but with the principalities, with the powers, with the world rulers of this present darkness, with the evil spirits in the heavens."[2]

These words of warning were not just for those days. If possible, they are more for now than for that time. The battle has been ongoing. The evil one has pulled out all the stops; he is savagely unleashing all the powers of hell to make his one last effort to destroy the Church of Jesus, to make God a liar, to drag as many of His children down to hell as he possibly can.

The Angels have been working overtime in this last

Are we aware of the Battle of the Angels?

century to ward off the attacks of Satan. There have been more accounts of Angelic intervention in the lives of the Faithful, to save them from hell.

But we are not even aware of all the battling that goes on behind the scenes if you will, between the powers and principalities, to save or destroy us. That's what this book is about. Cults have reared their ugly faces from the pits of hell in ways we have never considered possible. Their aim is to take all of us, but especially our young people, away from God, Church and family.

There are so many devils out there in the forms of friendly, smiling brothers and sisters, who want to separate us, divide us, keep us away from our support system in family and Church, so that we have no defenses against them. You will read in this book more instances of cults and sects who want to take us away from our Church, who want to offer us a new church, a church without Jesus, without the Cross, without our Mother Mary, our brothers and sisters the Saints, and our cousins the Angels.

You know, in your own life, there have been times when you have felt the intercession of the Heavenly Army of Angels. It might have been a voice in your heart, telling you to avoid a sinful situation. It may have been an overpowering feeling that you had to act on something to keep one of your children or a loved one out of physical or spiritual danger. You may have felt the need to pray for a loved one who was far away. You may have had a child who left home and you sent your Guardian Angel to the Angel of the child who might have been in danger.

In each of our books, we always have a Dedication. We really believe that it is most appropriate for this book to be dedicated to the Angels, our protectors, our soldiers who have been fighting for us all of our lives. Thank you Angels, for being for us; Thank You Jesus for giving us our Angels.

Footnotes

[1]Rev 12:7-8
[2]Eph 6:11-12

Glorify My Name...

Glorify My Name in all the World.

We would like to begin this book on Sects and Cults as we should begin all things, from morning to night, *In the name of the Father and of the Son and of the Holy Spirit.* Every time we hear these words, our minds and hearts fly to the Father in Heaven as He was creating the world, the Son Who chose to be born to die for our sins, and the Holy Spirit Who is always with us, inspiring us to be more so that someday we can dwell with the Holy Trinity in Heaven beholding the Beatific Vision. This is our Faith. This is what we say we believe, when we say *Amen.*

We awaken hearing the words ringing in our ears - *Glorify My Name throughout the world.* This book is partly about those who heard these words and, not having the guidance of an earthly father - our Popes, have set *themselves* up as Popes, perpetuating those who preceded them, and without really knowing what they were doing, have gone astray. This is also about those who, seeing problems and insidious cracks in the Temple, acted rashly and, putting themselves up as authorities, caused division upon division. And then there are those who sold their souls to Satan and have a plan to take as many of us down to the pits of hell with them, as they possibly can.

Jesus said *"A house divided against itself will fall."* This house, this Roman Catholic Church He founded, was so important to Him, He spent His every waking moment teaching and preparing those He was leaving behind how to be this visible Church on earth. From these twelve whom He commissioned[1] would come more and more - our Popes and Bishops, and from them our Priests, for 2000 years. This is part of our Deposit of Faith; this is the Church so many died for, so many live for. She is a glorious Church. We know this book is not supposed to be about Treasures of our church as we covered them in Trilogy Book I², but when we think of all the Graces that God wants to shower on *all* His children and they are blocked from finding out about them, we want to cry and instead we write!

The writing of this book has been a problem! With the first book of the Trilogy it was not easy but clear cut - the Treasures that make up the Church and separate us from our brothers and sisters in Christ; it was glorious writing that book; we were flying! The second book Trilogy Book II - *Tragedy of the Reformation* made us cry, as we walked through the lives of men who had been called to be apostles and had fallen. This book is different! It is a mixture of sects and cults, the guided and the misguided, victims and victimizers. They are all dangerous in one way or the other. But some are more dangerous than others. That is up to you to decide which if not all threaten you and your families.

When we began to write of sects, the question that haunted us was: How do we write with love, about the dedicated people who have given up their lives to serve the Lord through paths other than through the Catholic Church or Main-Line Protestant Religions? This chapter is not in any way a criticism of these brothers and sisters, only a story on how these different groups got started and what they teach that could lead unsuspecting Catholics and Protestants away from their churches.

This is also a book, we pray you will share not only with your families and your big Catholic family, but with our brothers and sisters in Christ and those who are flirting with sects or cults. Before we begin to speak of our differences, we want to share a letter we received from a theology student, preparing for ministry, attending *Oral*

Roberts University. This is our hope, our dream to bring all those who have wandered, back Home and those who are not with us through no fault of their own, into the family, the Mystical Body of Christ - the Catholic Church. How very much we love you!

Dear Bob and Penny:

*I just watched about the last half of Mother Angelica's program in which you were the guests. Enclosed please find a check for your book **"This Is My Body, This Is My Blood."** I am very much looking forward to reading your book. Also, I will be passing it along for others to benefit from.*

I want to share our testimony with you because I feel I know you somewhat after seeing you and hearing you on Mother Angelica's program. Certainly we are brothers and sisters in the Lord that shall meet when we go "Home."

I was raised a Methodist. My husband was raised a Pentecostal. We are now at Oral Roberts University, Tulsa, Oklahoma studying for the ministry. Both of us were raised in religiously prejudiced homes. One of the first things the Lord did after we committed our lives to Him was to break down denominational walls. We feel an ecumenical calling in our lives because our Lord is stressing to us the "strong" areas in each of the denominations of the Christian Church.

I want to share with you from the perspective of someone who was never a "Catholic," nor feels now a call to become a Catholic. I feel the Catholic Church has such tremendous potential for bringing to the Body of Christ (other denominations) a richer, fuller understanding of some scriptures and traditions, such as the Eucharist, as well as a better awareness of our Lord's sufferings and our own calling to be servants.

These are the things I admire:

1) There has been no compromise in the anti-abortion attitude - praise God!

2) There has been no lessening of the attitude of the sanctity of marriage. My husband and I were both married before and we know God has forgiven us. However, we believe the Church should stress and teach that marriage is a holy and lifelong union before God and not to be entered into lightly. Catholics ought to be the strongest pre-marriage counselors-teachers today.

3) Confessing to a priest. The Body of Christ may be calling out for revival but they have no idea of the humbling that occurs and the forgiveness that can happen when we confess our faults one to another. Please brothers and sisters in Christ who are Catholics, teach the Body about confessing our faults.

4) Thank you, that in the Catholic Church, I was visually confronted with Christ on the Cross. Of course, I know He is risen. But never seeing Him on the Cross, I never truly contemplated Him suffering and dying there. Then one day an ex-Catholic rather mockingly showed me an old book marker with Christ's picture. He was beaten; His Flesh was torn; it was truly terrible; it made me sick to my stomach. But I thank God that I saw our Lord like that and had to confront the pain and agony He went through for me. Isn't there some way the Catholic Church can cause the people of the world to "see" our Christ as He appeared on Good Friday? Couldn't the Catholic Church do an hour Television special over secular Television prime time on some Good Friday, in the future, and show Christ through various art forms and artists, how He suffered and died for us? Maybe it could be narrated and special classical music could be chosen to fit the sequence of pictures.

5). The beauty of the Eucharist. This teaching really needs to get into the Body of Christ. We need your help.

This letter has run on terribly - I apologize there is so much more you have to offer that we have noticed.

Just a personal note in closing. When my husband and I left the "business world" to answer God's calling our families were quite hostile to us. Except for Uncle Bill. He is my great Aunt's second husband and a Catholic. I don't believe he knows the Lord personally yet, because of his background he is pleased that someone in the family was called into the ministry. He sends us $500.00 per month to help support us.

Also another note. I am the eldest of four daughters and I was the first converted. My three younger sisters hated to be near me for sometime, but the Holy Spirit is successfully wooing them to Christ. The oldest of the three, one year ago married a Catholic man. He sponsored my sister as she attended classes to become a Catholic. She joined the Church on Good Friday and they both are now seeking the Lord's Will in their lives. How grateful to God I am, for a Catholic Church where my sister could meet Christ.

There are many people here at Oral Roberts University who were raised Catholics as children. They did not find Christ there, just as I did not find Him in my Methodist Church. We do not blame our churches any longer, for we know the fault was in us and in control of the Lord's timing. Many of the Catholics here are finding the Lord is calling them back to the Catholic Church.

I pray great blessings upon the Body of Christ in the Catholic Church. Hold fast to your confession of Faith.

I pray the Lord will use you mightily in bringing the Body together in the unity of the Spirit. You have so much to teach us.

Grace be multiplied unto you.

R. C.   *Tulsa, OK*

"*I pray the Lord will use you mightily in bringing the Body together in the unity of the Spirit.*" This unity that our sister closes her letter with, is the unity we seek, the Lord seeks and His Blessed Mother seeks. As we read in this letter, we can learn from one another, if we allow the Lord to touch our hearts. God wants His family to be one. And if we *cannot* all be under the Chair of Peter, as children of God we *can* all love one another.

Footnotes

[1]Matthias replaced Judas, the traitor, and became the twelfth.
[2]*Treasures of the Church - That which makes us Catholic*

Know your Faith or lose it!

The focus of this book is to let you know when you are being led astray from *without*. Those who proselytize against the Church are well prepared, conveniently using parts of the Bible, out of context - to confuse, to deceive, to convince, and to lead our children down that *wide path* to destruction which Jesus preached against. They boast about the millions and millions of dollars spent on teaching their members how to bring Catholics into their congregations.

In this book we are attempting to emphasize that if we are not to lose our families to Fundamentalist sects and more dangerously Cults, *we must know our Faith!* We must know so that we can not only evangelize but *defend* our Church from within as well as without.

When we wrote our book[1] on the heresies that have attacked our church over the last 2000 years, we spoke of the battle being raged *today*, Lucifer using all the heresies of the past in his ongoing effort to destroy Mother Church. Only now, he's *really* serious! Yes we have had times when most of our Bishops were Arian and not in union with the Holy See. We've had some really difficult situations where we had anti-popes and problem popes during the Renaissance period. But we have survived them; the good news is that the true Church of Jesus Christ, the Catholic Church is still here. Jesus has kept the promise He made to us, *"I will not leave you orphans," "The gates of hell will not prevail against My Church."* and *"I will be with you until the end of the world."* But it has not been easy-going. We find the enemy all around us, surrounding us, and yet we survive. We're wounded; we're sore; we'd like to take a couple of days off, but we know that's impossible.

Satan has become more devious, more cunning if that's possible. Today, the attacks are so devious, so all encompassing, we fear that one day we will awaken and find we are no longer Catholic. St. Jerome wrote that he feared one day he would awaken and find we were all Arian.[2]

If you take all the heresies we wrote about in **Trilogy Book I - Treasures of the Church**, and apply them to what is happening just in this last decade of the Second Millennium, you can't help but be aware that we're being bombarded with every weapon Satan has used down through the centuries, but now all at one time.

For instance, we believe in God; they[3] believe in "Ascended Masters." We believe in Angels; they believe in spirit guides. We believe in Resurrection; they believe in Reincarnation. We believe in being born again of the Holy Spirit; they believe in the law of Rebirth, which teaches that one is conditioned to believe that all wisdom is contained within oneself. But then, we believe the snake is a symbol of satan; they believe the snake is godlike. We believe 666 is demonic; they believe 666 is a religious symbol. We believe man is created in the Image of God; they believe man created God in his own image. We're not sure which man, and which image at this point, but you can be sure they'll tell us. It's a distortion of the truth; it's almost like... a parallel world.

Therefore, a good rule of thumb is, if it's confusing, it's not of the Lord. In the cult world, confusion reigns. In God's world, peace and joy reigns.

✻ ✻ ✻

One morning, prior to giving a talk before a group of women gathered under the banner of the *Magnificat*,[4] we went to Daily Mass. Let me go back a little. *First* we looked in the local telephone book for a Catholic Church in this little diocese which shall remain nameless. They say, Mother Mary's heart was pierced seven times,[5] but what we saw in this little diocese must have pierced her heart once again; the Catholic Church was listed as: *Catholic-Liberal,*

Catholic-Charismatic and *Catholic-Roman*. Dear God, we thought, what have they done with our *One, Holy, Catholic and Apostolic Church* - our Church which is Universal, the Church passed down by the first Apostles from Jesus Christ Himself? Are we no longer *one*? Is this not what we declare every time we make our Profession of Faith - our oneness? Is this not what our Lord prayed to the Father?

"...that all may be one as You, Father, are in Me, and I in You; I pray that they may be one in Us, that the world may believe that You sent Me."[6]

Is this not what we believe? Is this not what we promise to live by and if need be die for, every time we recite the Nicene Creed?[7] Is it not the Belief for which our Martyrs gave their lives? Did they not choose to die, rather than deny that which we have believed down through the ages?

Well we chose the *Catholic-Roman*. Everything was going fine; the priest even intoned *Kyrie, Eleison - Christe, Eleison - Kyrie, Eleison*, until we came to reciting the Lord's Prayer. He and the local daily communicants at Mass used the Protestant ending.[8] We weren't happy but it was not time to get devastated. The Eucharistic Prayer and the words of Consecration were all according to the Rubrics of the Church. Then it was time for the priest to distribute Holy Communion; only the priest handed the Ciborium filled with Consecrated Hosts to the parishioner in the front row (after giving him Communion), who then gave Communion to the person on his left, who proceeded to give the Eucharist to the person on her left and on and on. Row upon row, the Ciborium containing the Precious *Body, Blood Soul and Divinity* of Our Lord in His Eucharist was passed like a basket filled with so many wafers. We wanted to shout, along with Archbishop Fulton J. Sheen *"What have they done with my Lord?"* We were devastated!

Do we know our Faith? Do we really know anything about our Faith? Are we prepared to explain our Faith, no less defend it? Are we a part of our Church? Have we assumed responsibility for the evangelization of our Faith as required by virtue of our Baptism?

Do we apathetically stand by and say nothing, when we sense there is something wrong, as the Jews did the day Pilate asked *"Do you want me to release the King of the Jews?"* Or do we go along with the crowd and choose the one whom the world chooses - in their day an insurrectionist - in our day someone who is politically correct. Barabbas was politically correct in his time. Whom do we choose, today? We, in our travels, have heard that there are some more choices in *the new "do your own thing"* liturgies. A poor priest shared that he was told, by the Liturgical committee, that the congregation would play the part of Jesus and the priest the part of Peter during the reading of the Passion on Palm Sunday (or Passion Sunday as it has also been known) and Good Friday.

Are either of the instances we've described above correct? No! This plainly disregards the instructions in the front of the Sacramentary which state: The Passion can be read by the deacon and if he is not able by the laity. But *"The part of Christ if possible is reserved for the priest."* The priest is *In Persona Christi* not the laity. Now, we are telling the priest what part of the Passion he will play; what next? What part of the Sacramentary will we change next? Will the laity try to consecrate the host and the wine into the Body, Blood, Soul and Divinity of Jesus?

Does anyone have the right to change or ignore what is written in the instructions of the Roman Missal? No! We looked up the definition of the term "Rubrics:" *"Liturgical directives (instructions) found in the Roman Missal, including the Sacramentary and the Lectionary, which guide* **bishops, priests and deacons** *in the administration of the Eucharistic Sacrifice (the Mass), the Sacrament and Sacramentals, and the preaching of the Word* *of God.*" So neither bishops, priests nor deacons have the right to change the instructions in the Roman Missal. And definitely, not by any stretch of the imagination does any liturgical committee!

● Do we have the right to correct these errors?

● Do we have a responsibility to bring these errors to the attention of the proper people?

● Do we have an obligation to protect the people of God from these errors?

The answer to all of the above is a resounding *"yes!"* And now, the next natural question is *How do I find out what's right and what's wrong?* This brings us to the title of this chapter. *Know Your Faith or lose it!* You must learn what our Church teaches to defend yourself, your family and your Faith community from those who would spread errors in an effort to further an agenda which is not of the Lord, and subsequently not of the Catholic Church.

Is our Church perfect? Yes because she was left by Jesus Who is perfect. Are her shepherds always perfect? Sadly no; they are being perfected, just as the rest of us. The only difference is they have received extra *Grace* for their often very difficult walk. The battles fought and won are one of the clearest arguments that the Roman Catholic Church is the one founded by Jesus Christ. We have survived *2000 years* of attacks from within and without and we are still here! Praise God! Men and women from all walks of life have given their lives for this Church which Jesus founded. We are the only Church which can boast unbroken succession under the Chair of Peter. This is the foundation upon which we stand. Jesus is the Cornerstone of the Rock of Peter - the Roman Catholic Church.

We have been blessed either to be *born* into this glorious Church or of having received Jesus' invitation to come home to His Church. It is not a gift to be taken for granted, or to be ignored. We have to accept this gift from the Father, through our Lord Jesus Christ and the Holy Spirit, His magnificent Mother, our cousins, the Angels, and our brothers and sisters, the Saints. We must embrace the gift and we must pass it on.

Our job is to invite others to return to the Faith of their ancestors and to arm those who have remained - with the *Treasures of our Church* that they may defend this Bride of Christ against her enemies, that they may protect their children from being led astray.

Ours is not a Faith that can be learned by the eighth grade. We have been studying our Faith for the last 22 years, and we pray the Lord will allow us 22 more years to know more about God, and in knowing Him - love Him more, and in knowing and loving Him - serve Him more. Our Faith is inspiring; our History is exciting.

In this book, learn about Cults and Sects, groups who want to take you away from your Church. Learn why the Angels are on constant alert to battle with the powers that would destroy us.

Footnotes

[1] *Scandal of the Cross and its Triumph, Heresies throughout the History of the Church*

[2] Read about this heresy in our book *Scandal of the Cross and its Triumph, Heresies throughout the History of the Church* and see if we do not need to heed St. Jerome's words *today*!

[3] New Agers

[4] an outstanding movement of women faithful to the Magisterium and the Holy See. They are a support system and intercessory prayer group. In addition, they hold breakfasts four times a year inviting women to speak. If you do not have one in your community you should find out how you can start one.

[5] That does not mean 7 times literally but an infinite number of times.

[6] Jn 17:20-21

[7] another title for the Profession of Faith

[8] which is longer in the King James Bible

Christat or Crisis on Campus?

"Whatsoever you do to the least of My Children..."

Twenty-six years ago we lost a son to death through an overdose of drugs. That wound has never healed. Writing about it did not help, as we had to bring to the forefront those memories we had desired buried. After our son's death, when parents pleaded with us to pray for their children, we did pray, but then we went on with our lives. When we came back to Jesus and His Church, we offered Him all that we were or ever could be. We told Him we would do anything He asked of us *except* reach out to the young or console broken hearted parents who had lost children. If we have learned one thing, over the last twenty-two years, it is to not dictate to God *how* He is to use us. And so, we have taught young people in CCD for ten years and consoled grieving parents. Therefore, we were not ready when one day the Lord struck us with a four-by-four to the head and a sword to the heart.

What we discovered was that we are losing our young people when they leave home to continue their education. Whether in universities or colleges, whether secular or Catholic, often the story is the same: Our young, even from strong Catholic families, are being sucked up by cults! That's the bad news. The good news is we are reclaiming our young, calling them back to Jesus and the *only* Church He founded.

We have always felt that our mandate from the Lord was to evangelize to brothers and sisters who have left the Catholic Church, and to strengthen those who have remained, with the Treasures[1] we as Catholics have and believe in.

For some reason, we thought that our immediate families, our little churches, were all right. After all, we've taught our children and they've taught our grandchildren; and hopefully our brothers and sisters have taught our nieces and nephews. So when we go out to change the world, to do battle with the *enemy*, we don't consider our families, because we're sure our home bases are covered.

We go out like Don Quixote - to dream the impossible dream, to beat the unbeatable foe, content that those closest to us, our families, have solid foundations in the Faith, and are not under any great attack from the evil one. That's when we got hit right where it hurts - when we were rudely awakened through a loved one, a young loved one!

There is a crisis on campus and in the world, and we were to feel its full impact through a niece of one of our members of the ministry, Veronica, whose name means true icon. She is a good girl from a strong Catholic family. Even now, we remember the day she made her Quinceañera *(Among the Spanish-speaking people, a young woman makes her debut at 15 years old. Only these girls first consecrate themselves to the Lord through His Blessed Mother during the Mass.)* three short years ago, and how she looked when she walked down the aisle flanked by boys and girls, a royal court through which she processed to her Lord on the Altar. Unlike young women in the United States who come out at sixteen, and are presented at a ball, Veronica was first presented at the *Church*, and *then* at the reception. During the Mass, she walked over to the statue of the Blessed Mother, and leaving her a bouquet of flowers, she consecrated her chastity to Mother Mary for protection. She loved the Blessed Mother. She loved her Church.

She *believed*! Now at eighteen, she left home to live on campus, and within a couple of months she *no longer believed* all that her parents, and their parents, and their parents before them have passed down for the last 500 years since Our Lady of Guadalupe appeared in Mexico in 1531. It was only by the Grace of God that we discovered she had left the Church. It was the old story: When she arrived on campus, no Catholics befriended her! The only ones who reached out to her were young people trying to get her to go to their church, insisting after all, it was *non-denominational* (actually their church was Church of Christ which is non-denominational, except when it comes to their interpretation of the Bible). At first, she refused, insisting she was Catholic and attended the Catholic Church. *Then* they asked her if she would like to grow closer to Jesus. When she said *Yes!* they asked her if she would like to go to a non-denominational Bible Study with them. It sounded safe and she was on her way to becoming a member of a cult!

We found out about it through her younger cousin who began to attend this non-Catholic church with Veronica because she looked up to her cousin; *besides they were such nice people!* Thank God, Veronica requested to speak with her aunt at the Ministry; she spent quite a bit of time on the phone, openly sharing her newly-acquired doubts. We invited Veronica to visit us in Sacramento.

She came up with a Protestant Bible which her new-found *friends* had given her. They even had the Bible hot-stamped with her name! She told us that she had gotten caught up in the college life when she first entered and it was a new and exciting experience. People embraced her and reached out to her. *They were not Catholic*, but at first they did not seem to be *anti-Catholic*. They were Biblical, which put her mind at rest; after all, Catholics are Biblical. She wanted to learn more about Jesus; so when her friends invited her to go to their Bible Study, she did, and when she heard the eloquent preaching, she was hooked.

Then her newfound friends began criticizing Catholics

as not being Scriptural. She was not aware that their interpretation of what constitutes Scripture is quite different from ours. Ours is based on the teachings of the Church and our Traditions dating back 2000 years. Theirs is based on individual interpretation. This group turned out to be very anti-Catholic. But as we found out, when we researched this particular group, they were anti every faith belief but their own; however, Catholics were at the top of the list. They had been able to easily put doubts into her young mind, because of her love for Jesus and her yearning for a personal relationship with Him.

She needed someone to tell her, we as Catholics not only have a personal relationship with Jesus, when we receive Him, He consumes us and we no longer live but Jesus lives through us. But she did not know where to turn for help addressing the doubts that had been placed in her mind and heart. She needed soldiers on campus to help her arm herself and strengthen her faith. She had not been made aware of the Catholic Ministry which exists on campus, and she didn't know how to go about finding young people of her own Faith, so she had joined those who had reached out to her.

We answered all the pat tract questions with which *friendly* proselytizing students had indoctrinated her (another word would be brainwashed). This cult of non-denominational Fundamentalists had been challenging her about some of the teachings of the Catholic Faith, especially *Communion, Confession, Purgatory, the Pope and our devotion to our Mother Mary*, prefacing each question with, *"Where is that in Scripture?"* and *"Where did the Church find justification for this or that practice or belief?"* As we heard this sweet soul who had always loved the Church even questioning *Mary*, we couldn't believe our ears. *Not Mary!* After all, her family is originally from Mexico and when she was baptized, Veronica (like all Mexican babies) was presented to the Mother of God a*s her child* and then Mary was introduced to Veronica as *her Mother*. Now, this little girl was questioning her Heavenly Mother - her Lady of Guadalupe, and all that she and her family had held dear for generations!

We invited a very special missionary priest to our home to join us for lunch, but more importantly to help our young friend. Veronica would gently throw out one of their questions, and following our priest's lead we would pause and silently pray for inspiration from the Holy Spirit, before we answered. We were able to answer all her questions to her satisfaction, careful not to condemn her friends; after all, they were sincere in what they believed.

[It really is not as complex or as difficult as most think, as most former Protestants, who tried to find justification *not* to believe will tell you that the *Word* affirms all that the Catholic Church teaches. When the Bible further pointed to the irrefutable fact that the Catholic Church is the one true Church founded by Christ Himself, they knew they had to go Home and they converted.]

Veronica did not want to leave her Church! She had just wanted to get closer to Jesus. She was now convinced that she was part of the One, True Church - the *Roman Catholic Church*, which could bring her not only closer to Jesus but give her the precious Sacraments that would unite her eternally to her Savior.

We bought her a *Catholic* Bible and showed her the wonderful seven books of the Old Testament missing in Protestant Bibles. She left the Protestant Bible her friends had given her behind with us. She was at peace! She had only one dilemma and that was what would she say to the dear people who had befriended her. Our priest prayed for a moment and then replied: *"When you return to campus, tell them how, before you went to the university, you had a strong foundation of the Faith, and when you met them they were responsible for awakening a deeper knowledge of Jesus for which you thank them; but now you want to grow closer to Jesus through your own Church.* "

Veronica said, with all due respect, what impressed her the most was Father Ryan taking the time to be with her, as she knew this was the day before he was leaving our parish to return to the Missions in Africa. Like Jesus, with so little time, he thought of her and her soul. The other thing that affected a change in her was her mother. She kept repeating over and over again, *"I made my mother cry. I can never forgive myself for making my mother cry."*

At Christmas time Veronica had shared with her mother that she was going to another church. She said *"Look around you. Our home is filled with family members, all talking but not about Jesus. Soon we'll all congregate and eat our Christmas dinner and open our gifts. But there will be no mention of what this holiday is all about - Our Lord Jesus Who was born to save the world."* Her mother cried, wiped her tears and then called everyone to come into the dining room. She turned to her family and said, *"It has been brought to my attention that we do not even pray before eating our meal on this holy day, so I want to ask everyone to hold hands and thank Jesus for being born by beginning with the Lord's Prayer and then the Hail Mary giving thanks to His Mother Mary for saying yes; because without her there would not have been any Christmas."* She said she needed someone to open her eyes to how far they had gone away from the Truth they had learned and treasured. She did not mention her daughter's name, but the girl knew. It meant so much to her!

Before Veronica left us, she repeated she could never forgive herself for making her mother cry. The priest took this moment to affirm her and the miracle that took place within the whole family because she was open to her mother's broken heart; Jesus had truly been born that day - in her home, in her family's heart. Unlike the inn in Bethlehem, there was a room for Jesus in this home.

We contacted the Catholic Campus Ministry at her university, and found out how she could get involved with other Catholic young people on campus. She went back to the university, armed with her own copy of the Catholic Bible, the Catholic Catechism, *and* our books and videos. She looked like Saint Joan of Arc, in battle dress, ready to reach out to all Catholics on Campus and share what she had learned this weekend.

Veronica five months later...

We hadn't seen Veronica for five months, but we never stopped praying for her. I can't explain why, but we couldn't stop praying, even though we knew she was resolved to go back to her Church. I guess, again the Holy Spirit was speaking to our hearts. She told us that when she had returned to the campus, and explained her decision to remain in the Catholic Church, her fundamentalist friends turned her off! Then two weeks later, one of them called and invited her to come to a Bible Study. She thanked her from the bottom of her heart but said no, again! A few days later, a very nice young man, whom she had met at the Church of Christ services, approached her on campus. How was she doing? Everyone, especially he missed her; they all had been wondering what had happened to her. Now this is a small intimate group and he did not know she was no longer going to attend?

Then he said he had heard she was going back to the Catholic Church. She replied yes and told him exactly what she had told the girl - that although she thanked them for bringing her closer to Jesus, she was going to continue to find Him in her own Church. Then she made a mistake! She told him how she could never forgive herself for making her mother cry! That's all he needed! She had, without knowing, left the door open, as St. Teresa said for the enemy to slither in, and slither in he did. *"I know what you are going through, but you will be back! You are only staying with the Catholic Church out of loyalty to your mother. You know that you really belong in our church, because that is where Jesus is. My father is a minister and I had to leave him and my mother. You have to heed what Jesus said about leaving mother and father for the kingdom!" "Boy"* I said, *"He really thinks you are stupid to be taken in by that manipulation!"* Is his father a minister? I hope so, so he does not have another strike against him. I must admit I was upset!

They never let up, and we cannot let up. They believe in something that wounds Jesus' heart, and they never let up. We who love Him and are blessed to be part of His Church, can we do less? I don't know why I was so upset. Hadn't the same thing happened to us, thirty years before, with our son? Two weeks after our son Richard entered the University of California, Los Angeles, he came home and told us there was no God. And this was from a young man who had gone to *Catholic* Grammar School, and then *Catholic* High School, the finest Jesuit School in Southern California. He was head of the Church Youth group at Our Lady of Malibu Church. Who would ever have thought that such a strong Catholic could be coerced and brain-washed by outside forces? But he was overpowered by his new environment, and the pressures that were pulling at him from all sides.

We knew of no Campus Ministry on campus reaching out to Catholics, and so we were powerless to help our own son, our knowledge of the Faith at that time inadequate to handle the very clever manipulation of his professors' paganistic Philosophy. He found his friends within his fraternity, which in the 60's was completely godless, more involved in drugs and parties than in defending God.

Now it was thirty years later and we thought everything was better, and it had happened to one of our own's niece. We went into action, because we knew she could still get swallowed up. We knew we had to do whatever we could to insure that she wasn't left alone without any support. We remembered how helpless we felt when this had happened to our son in college.

What is our part? What can we do?

Not just us, but *all* of us. What are we doing to hold on to our Catholic boys and girls who go off to college? A priest once told us that the Catholic Church was the only Church who stopped educating their flock when they left High School. There's no follow up when they enter college, and even less when they become adults. A great deal of attention is given to our Catholic children of Grammar School and High School age. But we seem to be remiss when it comes to our college youth. Either we think they're at an age where they can take care of themselves when it comes to matters of the Faith, or we don't think they'll be subjected to that type of pressure, or we just have too many other priorities of our own, such as paying their tuition, room and board. *Or worse, we just don't know.*

Brothers and sisters, we have a great deal of work to do. There are such war stories coming out of our educational systems. The enemy knows that this is a perfect time to come down on our young people. They've been under supervision and regimentation for at least twelve years of their school life. Now, all of a sudden the disciplines have been removed. They're away from home, parental supervision, Church and etc. They don't know how to handle it, but the enemy does. He lurks in the shadows, just waiting to jump out and attack, and very often, we never get them back. We can't let that happen. The way they are suckered into these cults are by challenges. And as in the case of this young woman a desire to know more about Jesus. It's usually the sensitive children who are the most easily influenced by the cults. They're the ones they want. They know that the students are searching for something more. They're looking for God. What can we do about it?

We spoke to a director of Campus Ministry

We spoke to the Campus Ministry Director of a state with one of largest populations in the U.S. He told us the only way they can reach a student, getting ready to go off to College, is through cooperation from Catholic High Schools, Parish Churches, and *parents*. He sends out a packet each year to every *Catholic High School* in the state, requesting that this kit be copied and given to seniors who are preparing to graduate. The school is asked to send the names of future college students and the colleges they will attend to his office. In this way, campus ministries in the individual colleges will receive the list and become aware of new Catholic students arriving on their campuses. It will also enable *members* of the Campus Ministry to contact Catholic students, *when they first arrive*, and assist entering students to know and meet other Catholic students on campus. Barely 60% of the Catholic Schools cooperate.

We were told that to reach students who go to *public schools* is more difficult. The kit is sent to each *Parish* in the state, requesting students be advised of the kit, instruct them to fill them out, and return them to the Parish, or directly to the Campus Ministry office. The response is very weak on the Parish level, and this is the area where the greatest amount of students going to public colleges can be reached.

Our last hope is you parents

Our Popes, and the *Declaration on Christian Education* included in the Vatican Council II documents clearly states that we parents are primarily responsible for the education of our children. Your job, as parents, is to speak to the Catholic School - if your child goes to a Catholic School, and request they give these packets out to not only your child, but to all seniors. If your child goes to Public High School, contact your Parish, and ask whoever is responsible, whether it be the Director of Religious Education, or the Pastor, or the secretary to get these kits out to the seniors graduating. If your parish doesn't have the kits, contact the Campus Ministry office in your diocese, and ask them to send the kits to your home.

Most importantly, parents, tell your children to be on the lookout for this material from the Campus Ministry office of your diocese; ask the Catholic High School if your children go there, or the Parish office if your child goes to a public school, and if none of that works, call the Campus Ministry and ask them to send the kit to your home.

Make sure your child is not left alone when he or she gets to college for the first time. Go with your child, initially and make sure his soul as well as his mind is going to be nourished. Remember, you've spent all these years protecting your child from the powers of evil. Now that your child is out of your physical control, don't let the devil get to this precious child on campus. It's your job, its our job; for every child is our child and when one dies, in one way or another, the world is poorer. This chapter is dedicated to the two girls who made it and to one young man who didn't.

We love you.

Christ on Campus

We went looking for answers, at the *Franciscan University of Steubenville.*

This whole experience really hit home! When Veronica was almost taken in by the young members of that cult, it brought back those painful memories of our son. But God never wastes anything, especially crosses. We knew we had to do something! We had come so close to losing Veronica, a dear and most precious soul, we began our search for answers.

Bob & Penny with students at Franciscan University

We made a trip to the *Franciscan University of Steubenville.* Our quest was to find out how we could bring Jesus to Catholic students on secular campuses in the United States and the world. We knew of this University; we had seen the fruits when we worked with their alumni out in the world; but we had to go there, to walk among them, to experience the electricity that was generated on campus, the peace and joy that permeated the student body through the ongoing presence of Jesus alive on campus.

We have a saying in our ministry that our Chairman of the Board is Jesus. Well as we walked the grounds of this campus and interviewed students and professors, it is obvious that the power behind every breath these young people take is their love for the Lord Who dwells there.

On this campus, we found no *head without heart philosophy* that fails to fulfill the yearning in the human spirit, nor *heart without head emotionalism* that soon chills in the cold reality of the outside world. Here we met the true living out of the Gospel - the unity of one mind, one heart, one spirit. You could not fail to perceive and experience the fire of the Holy Spirit which rises from the swells of this Mystical Body of Christ - professors and students alike. As we roamed the rolling hills of the campus we could see the hustle and bustle of students rushing to class, not unlike that which we would experience on any campus. But the difference was the variety - priests, sisters, brothers, friars, lay professors, students from the youngest to the more mature - undergraduates and post graduates. Coming from more than 45 countries, you see a mixture of colors, diverse cultures and varied backgrounds. Yet these 1,964 students form *family*! We needed to know what makes them one.

We interviewed those who had transferred from other universities, and all their testimonies led to one blazing need for evangelization on campus. One student spoke of her experiences on a campus in the midwest whose student body numbered 60,000. She said it was very quiet there, with no distractions, as students passed each other without acknowledging each other. No one spoke to her; no one, that is, until she walked onto the quadrangle in the center of the campus. There friendly faces reached out to her, inviting her to their Bible Classes. She was lonely and felt the aloneness that being just another number on campus can bring. She didn't care who they were; they were friendly and loving; she was away from home and this was what she needed.

But the time came when these well-meaning brothers

and sisters started to attack all that she had believed in - the Eucharist, Mother Mary, Purgatory, the Papacy, and on and on. She wept as she was told that Mary was not a virgin and that she had other children. She began to question their Christianity as they called the Church - the Whore of Babylon and the Pope - the antichrist. Her pain became too much to bear when they attacked her belief that Jesus is truly Present in the Eucharist - Body, Blood, Soul and Divinity, but instead they contend the Host is merely a symbol.

But they were the only ones who befriended her! Whereas at first she was wounded, soon she was approaching other Catholics, repeating by rote the same tract questions her new-found friends had used on her. When she finally discovered they were solely using her to discredit the Faith,

Bob & Penny Lord with
Fr. Michael Scanlan
President of the Franciscan University at
Steubenville, Ohio

and were intolerant bordering on unloving when she questioned some of their beliefs, she left them. She was more fortunate than many others who had fallen prey to these well-prepared proselytizers. Years later, she grieved with an ongoing pain, wondering how many dead bodies she had left behind, those who still believed all they had now made their own.

We greeted each day with the sight of students and faculty attending Mass either at 6:30 a.m., 12 noon, or 6:30 p.m. Father Michael Scanlan, the president of the university, told us attendance at Mass is strictly voluntary. *And the* chapel was mobbed! We attended all three masses and the truth is they were all full! We had to arrive fifteen minutes before Mass started, to get seats. The students and staff were there praying! When the Mass was over, no one got up; they remained praying, offering praise and

Replica of the Portziuncola at Franciscan University of Steubenville

thanksgiving to the Lord Who had come to them, bringing them new life!

As we wandered around the very peaceful campus, we could not fail to spot students walking toward a little stone chapel. On the hill, looming above the trees was a symbol of *the Poor One*, St. Francis of Assisi, an exact replica of the Portziuncola that is in Santa Maria Degli Angeli in Assisi - the first church of St. Francis and his friars. There is an ongoing array of students entering this little House of God. What attracts them? They know that within, Jesus in His Most Holy Sacrament is waiting for them. As we entered the *little portion,* another name for the Portziuncola, there was a hush, a serenity, a wave of gentle but powerful holiness filling the tiny chapel, and the memories of days and years spent in the Portziuncola in Assisi came rushing back to us.

Our eyes fell on the only light cutting through the soft shadows - it was *the Light* and those present had no doubt *Who* that Light was - Our Lord resplendent on His Throne in a monstrance, hidden under the appearance of a piece of bread, but bread no longer, their King waiting vulnerably for them. We knelt, quietly wrapped in the awe and wonder of this God Who had such power to reach these young people. All around us were students deep in prayer; in the silence of their heart speaking and then listening to their Lord.

We believe in Our Lord present in the Eucharist; we know that hell will not prevail against the Lord's Church; but there are times, when we see all the attacks on the Church from without and within, we need to witness the faith we encountered in these young people. They reinforced our hopes and dreams for the Roman Catholic Church in the United States and in the world. Pope John Paul II said they are the Church of *today*. We see them also as the hope of *tomorrow* - for the Church, for our country, for our world.

There is a joy on this campus that is contagious. You hear it through the songs and praise that are lifted up to the Lord at Mass. Never sacrificing the reverence due His Majesty, the young were alive with the Holy Spirit flowing from the altar to them, and then through them to one another, and then to those of us who were blessed to be among them. As we knelt and expectantly awaited the sweet kiss of Jesus (St. Therese, the Little Flower *and* our newest *Doctor of the Church*, called her First Holy Communion her first kiss from Jesus), it was as if David were there, dancing as he did when the Arc of the Covenant was being processed into the Holy Tent. Only now, there were hundreds of young Davids and the dancing was in their hearts.

Boredom at Mass? Do we hear that our youth are bored at Mass? Not these young people! What is the difference? Why are they not bored? Why are they so alive? Why do they take precious time from their studies and social life to spend time with their Lord adoring Him in the Blessed Sacrament? Why go to Mass each day? Do they have that clear sense they are walking with Christ to His Cross, beside Him as He offers Himself to the Father once again through the ongoing Sacrifice of the Cross, the Sacrifice of the Mass?

Is this why, in a world where there is purported a crisis in vocations to the Priesthood, there are over 120 men discerning the priesthood on this campus?

What is the difference? A priest recently told us you do not have to know the Sacraments to receive them. Father I understand, but to know the value of the Gift we must know what it is and what place it can play in our lives. These students know their Church and they love her. Because they do know, they will make holy Priests, holy Brides of Christ, Nuns and Sisters, holy men and women consecrated to the Lord - whether through the celibate life or the Sacrament of Matrimony.

An alumni from this university, who was teaching high school, once told us that before he could teach his students about the Eucharist, he had to first teach them about Jesus. We thought about this. How can we feel passionately about the Eucharist, Our Lord Who comes to us under the appearance of bread and wine, if we do not *know* the Jesus - the God-Man Who was born and Who died that we might never die? What is the difference between these young people and those who are led astray by cults? Knowledge of the Lord and the Church He founded! No mature responsible human being would leave his country for an unknown country with a different language before knowing *first* what his country had to offer and then what the new land had to offer.

Our Pope has asked us to consider our young as a part of a new and different society - a people to be recognized and respected. As with our ancestors who came from different cultures and had to learn about this culture which makes up the people of the United States, so today we have to learn about the culture of our children - this new generation, so that as our ancestors before us, we can marry the new with the old and form a strong family in Christ and

His Church.

We see the beginning of a *Gentle Revolution*. We see in our travels, not only in this country but around the world, Our Lord and His Mother gathering up soldiers for the battle ahead - love and knowledge of our Faith their armor and shield. We, the Mystical Body of Christ are a chosen people called to a royal priesthood by virtue of our Baptism. We have been mandated by our Lord, and all the successors of St. Peter our first Pope, to go out to all the world and evangelize to the lambs who have strayed, and to strengthen, arm and call forth those who have remained to join the battle. Put on the armor of God! We are in the most glorious days of the Church. More and more people are realizing what is missing in their lives is God.

We have over 100,000 converts coming into the Catholic Church each year, and that makes the Father in Heaven so very happy. But the Hearts of Jesus and Mary are pierced each time one of their children, baptized Catholic, leave Home - leaves the Faith of their fathers - the Roman Catholic Church. Whose responsibility is it to protect the innocent lambs of God? Who will be held accountable for every soul who could have been touched by word or deed? Every soul is a soul created by God and therefore precious to the Father in Heaven. When we stand before the throne of God, how will we respond when Jesus says, *I chose you to be an instrument of hope - a bridge for the lost to cross over to the one true Church, but you were too busy?*

This is our Church. We belong to the family of God. Every child is our child. Each child of God lost to the Catholic Church puts another thorn on Jesus' Heart, makes our Church the poorer, makes us weaker. We have put aside our fears and wounds to write this book. In our own family, we painfully learned, if you do not change the world the world will change you. When our son entered a secular university, after a matter of a few weeks of philosophy, he came home and said: *There is no God.* We were helpless because we did not know how to wage war on this enemy which had invaded our home and our life. But now we know, and we are determined to stop the *father of lies* from killing any more children, from robbing them of their God and then their lives; no more are to be lost to Our Lord, as long as we have a breath left in our body.

✝

Who lives?
If your answer is Jesus Christ and Mother Mary,
pick up your banner
and follow our Sweet Christ on Earth.[2]

Footnotes

[1]Read *Treasures of the Church - That which makes us Catholic -* by Bob and Penny Lord.
[2]what St. Catherine of Siena called all Popes

Anatomy of a Cult

Impending Danger

We want to begin this chapter by giving you a definition of Cults. When a given group breaks away from an established church, and begins preaching heresies which are against the teachings of Christianity, they fall into the category of cults. For instance, if they deny the Trinity, or the Divinity of Jesus, or the teachings of the Old Testament, they would be considered cults.

A major cause of breaks between groups and established churches is interpretation of the Bible. This has caused so much division and dissension, since John Wycliff and Martin Luther encouraged individual interpretation of Scripture. It has caused rifts that have developed into Cults and Sects. In this chapter, we're going to concentrate on those whose interpretation has been so against the teachings of the Church and Christianity as a whole, they have to be categorized as Cults.

Cults can also be categorized as being any group that uses another source in addition to, or in place of Holy Scripture as their Spirit Guide. Most of the cults we will be sharing in this chapter fit into that category. Very often, the break with organized or established religion is so severe, the cult does not consider their history beginning with Jesus or with the Creation, but with the founding of the particular cult. Many teach that religion took a break from the time of Jesus until the time the cult was organized, that the Holy Spirit stopped working in the Church from the end of the Book of Revelation to the beginning of the particular cult.

Within the framework of cults, there are what are called *"Destructive Cults:"*

"A destructive cult (or sect) is a highly manipulative group which exploits and sometimes physically and/or psychologically damages members and recruits.

"A destructive cult:

a)dictates - sometimes in great detail - how members should think, feel and act;

b)claims a special exalted status (i.e. occult powers; a mission to save humanity) for itself and/or its leaders - which usually sets it in opposition to mainline society and/or the family;

c)exploits its members psychologically, financially, and/or physically;

d)utilizes manipulative or 'mind control techniques,' especially for the denigration of independent critical thinking, to recruit prospects and make members loyal, obedient, and subservient; and

e)causes considerable psychological harm to many of its members or to its members' families."[1]

Our original purpose, when we used this definition of a cult, was not to frighten or alarm you. Nor is it that the intent of the authors of that definition. They maintain that all cults or sects are not necessarily destructive, even if they are heretical. But there *are* degrees of destruction. Does not heresy lead you away from the Truth and the Church to whom Jesus left His Treasures, that we would have eternal life with Him? It is good for you to be concerned about groups that you allow yourselves or members of your family to become involved in, and to consider the possible consequences of that involvement, before flirting dangerously with something about which you know *nothing*. As a matter of fact, any cult or sect which could take you away from Jesus, your Church and your family, is dangerous![2]

Although there have always been dangerous cults, beginning with the 40's, they have become more numerous and have wielded greater influence as the years have gone by. Because they are so devious, they have drawn millions of innocent lambs into their dens of disorder, destruction and often death, with five thousand destructive cults in the United States totaling *three to five million* members. And to our deep sadness, they say that thirty-five to fifty percent of their membership are former Catholics, a few of them who still keep ties with the Church.

It is difficult to lump all groups under one common title, whether that of Cults, Sects, or Denominations, therefore read what we have discovered of the different groups included in this book and make your own evaluation. We have just chosen a few to try to give you an idea of the present and impending danger to our families, our Church, our country, our world.

We are expressing the need for caution, as there have been lunatic groups we have been hearing about lately who have talked their followers into committing mass suicide. We shouldn't take anything for granted, or put anything past anyone who claims exalted powers of any kind. Another good rule of thumb is that anyone who would separate us from Jesus and His Church is not good for us.

Although in the Twentieth Century 90% of all Protestants have belonged to the Main-Line Religions, the cults have been making dangerous inroads, leading astray our brothers and sisters in Christ as well as those in our Catholic Family. We want to describe them by date and time so that we can see how the Cross of Christ has been fractured by one splinter after the other breaking off from the Tree (the Church) for whom Christ gave His Life. Oh how wounded He must be to see His children divided, His

Lambs being led into a den of false teachings.

We can see what a danger they pose not only to our Church, but to our country. In our first two books of this Trilogy, we focused on what separates us from main-line Protestant brothers and sisters, and how we pray we can be united. This book should be read by Catholics and Protestants alike. It shows graphically how we're being picked off by forces outside of Christianity, who are very professional and forceful in their methods of recruiting and maintaining their flock, once they've stolen loved ones from our families. We're told by professionals who work at rescuing young people from cults, into which they have become entrapped, that it's far easier to keep them out of these cults in the first place than it is to try to get them out once they're in.

CULTS

1774 - **The Unitarian Church** - throwbacks to Arianism

When they began, Unitarians could have been rightly labeled *throwbacks to Arianism*. Their main thrust was a *denial of the Trinity*, thus the name *Uni*, meaning one. They do not believe there are three persons in the Trinity, only Jesus.[3]

They were first heard of in Europe about the time of Luther and Calvin. Their mentor, a *Michael Servetus*, wrote a paper entitled *"On the Errors of the Trinity,"* which he presented to Luther and Calvin with the hope it would be supported by them. They dashed all Servetus' hopes; they condemned him as a blasphemer. He tried to open a dialog with Calvin to no avail. And what did Calvin do, if he did not accept someone else's doctrines? While Servetus was passing through Geneva, he was captured by Calvin's men and burned at the stake. So much for the Unitarians in Europe. They suffered much persecution until they relocated in England.

The Unitarian Church in England was founded by a dissident from the Congregationalist faith, Theophilus Lindley, in London, in 1774. This religion is considered a cult, not part of the Main Line Protestant religions. Their concepts and beliefs are outside the Bible, in that they do not acknowledge the Triune God - *The Holy Trinity*. Because of this, they are separated from the Truth that Christ taught and left. They also *reject Original Sin, Atonement for sins*, and *Eternal punishment*.

In researching this cult, we discovered that Unitarians do not practice *any* of their original concepts today. So what their founder, Servetus died for, is considered basically rubbish by those who have followed him. They have become *"enlightened."* A Unitarian scholar and historian, Earl Morse Wilbur wrote of the modern Unitarian movement:

*"When the Unitarian movement began, the marks of true religion were commonly thought to be belief in the creeds, membership in the church, and participation in **its** rites and sacraments. To the Unitarian of today the marks of true religion are spiritual freedom, enlightened reason, broad and tolerant sympathy, upright character and unselfish service. These things, which go to the very heart of life, best express the meaning of Unitarian history."[4]*

American Unitarians now fall more into the category of *Humanism - I believe in man?* [I remember what we were taught, if you hear anyone say they believe in man, it is the enemy of God speaking through him. Now, I am not saying Unitarians are necessarily enemies of God, but let us look at what they now believe.]

Whereas they first believed in only One Person - Jesus the One God, rather than in the Holy Trinity[5] (which in itself would qualify them for the title - Cult), they now reject that as well. The Unitarians in the Midwest and the West could easily be ranked *agnostics*. They reject any orthodox beliefs their cult held in the past, a small number still believing in Jesus Christ as their personal God, in the Bible as the Word of God, and in immortality (eternal life after death). And if you still have a problem with us calling them a cult, they do not believe Jesus is God - but that he is one of *many*

Thomas Jefferson

religious teachers, and rank Christianity with Buddhism, Hinduism, Islam and etc.

"I trust that there is not a young man living in the United States who will not die a Unitarian." - Thomas Jefferson, our third President whose dream was that the Unitarian Religion would be the national religion of the United States. Although he was not to realize that in his generation or those to come, this country would have its destiny formed by Unitarians throughout our existence. No religious denomination has had as many prominent figures in the United States as the *Unitarian Universalists.*[6] The Roll Call begins with *five* Presidents of the United States: *John Adams, John Quincy Adams, Thomas Jefferson, Millard Fillmore,* and *William Howard Taft.* One Unitarian whose name never

John Adams

made it in this Hall of Fame was *Adlai Stevenson* who ran for office, but was never elected President.

In a nation with about 1/10 of 1% of the population having (at this writing) the greatest representation of any other denomination, with 3 Unitarians serving in the Senate and 8 in the House of Representatives, versus with Catholics being 24% of the population having totally 13 senators,[7] what does that say about our fair representation as Catholics? And I wonder how many there are today, out of that number who really belong to the Catholic Church? By their vote on issues clearly against our beliefs, it leads us to conjecture, maybe we are not Unitarians, but are we living in a Unitarian society? With all the hullabaloo and fuss about *John Kennedy* being a Catholic, in his administration, there were two top posts held by Unitarians: *Arthur Schlesinger, Jr.* and *Ted Sorenson.*

1783 - The Swedenborgians

The Swedenborgians are a little-known cult which was actually instituted unofficially by a *scientist* turned *spiritualist* - Emmanuel Swedenborg. He was considered brilliant, having received a Ph.D. when he was barely 21 years old. He wrote more than 60 books and pamphlets on Science; but at age 55 he turned his attention wholly to the promulgation of the *spirit world.* He led people to believe that he had been granted power to live both in the terrestrial[8] *an*d the celestial[9] world. In his first 29 volumes *in Latin* on *spiritualism*, he covered what he alleged *life in the spirit world.* Like so many self-appointed theologians and prophets, within and without the One True Church, he even pridefully delivered his *own* bizarre rendering of the Gospel.

He described his encounters with the spiritual world, quoting from claimed out-of-world discussions he had with St. Paul, Luther, the Popes, Moslems, believers and infidels alike. Not satisfied with that contradictory mixture of bedfellows, he added his dialogues with the angels. [Which angels - God's Heavenly Army of Angels or Lucifer's army of fallen angels?]

As like other cults before and after him, he rejected not only the teachings of the Roman Catholic Church but those of Main-Line Protestant religions (including the Lutheran Church where his father had been a bishop). An interesting aside; he rejected Luther's doctrine of Justification by Faith alone, as had his father, the Lutheran bishop. Among other attacks on the beliefs of most Christians, he contradicted most emphatically the Trinity.

His main claim to fame was that he was a *seer*. He wove preposterous tales of visions (he claimed to have witnessed the Last Judgment which took place in 1757). The Swedes loved him. He shared that he had to stop attending services at the State Lutheran Church because he claimed his spirit friends disrupted the sermons and disagreed with the preacher. (Do you ever wonder if some of these alleged seers are suffering from some kind of mental illness, hearing voices?) To quote those who knew Emmanuel Swedenborg, they believed that his visions were manifestations of a mental disease (*paranoia*).[10] To quote John Wesley, founder of the Methodist Church, *"he* (Swedenborg) *was one of the most ingenious, lively, entertaining madman that ever set pen to paper."*[11]

He never founded a Church. But he did have a theology of sorts. He maintained that after we die, we enjoy a *spirit life* very similar to that which we experienced on earth. At some given time, (not indicated) each person will go to where he/she will feel most comfortable. It could be Heaven, the spirit world (Purgatory?) or hell. We humans will not be the only ones in Heaven, hell or wherever. We will share with creatures of other planets. In addition, our marriages will continue eternally, but the partners could be somewhat different, especially in the case of someone who has had many spouses.

He also came up with a bible of sorts, using codes for various objects in the bible, such as: stones meaning truth; houses meaning intelligence; snakes meaning carnal (we call it concupiscence[12]); cities were religious systems and so on.

Somebody else founded a Church based on the writings of Swedenborg! Eleven years after his death, this cult was formed by an English printer and some Anglican clergy in 1783. It was called the *New Jerusalem Church*. They ordained ministers and formed a proper organization. In 1789 they had enough chapters to form a conference, and then, naturally, they brought it to the United States in 1792. Swedenborg has always been considered their guru, or as one congregation put it, "*the heaven-sent revealer of the true spiritual meaning of Scripture.*" He has also been described by his followers as "*a divinely illuminated seer and revelator.*"

As God always saves His lambs, membership in this cult is diminishing and his writings are virtually unknown by Christians.

1820 - The Mormon Church

This cult[13] is also called, **Church of Jesus Christ of Latter Day Saints**. It was begun by Joseph Smith in Palmyra, New York in the year 1827. Joseph Smith asserted he had had a vision of an angel called Moroni, in 1820. For more information on this cult, see the chapter on Mormons in this book.

1830 - The **Disciples of Christ**[14] (**The Church of Christ**)
"Study your Bible and believe what you wish."

This cult was formed by Thomas Campbell who left Ireland and settled in the United States. Thomas began as a preacher in the Presbyterian Church in western Pennsylvania. Because of his unorthodox practices of inviting those outside the church to receive communion, he was asked to leave and began a nondenominational church in Washington County, Pennsylvania. His son Alexander arrived from Ireland and joined his father as an on-call preacher. They preached with the authority: *"Where the Scriptures speak, we speak; where the Scriptures are silent, we are silent."* Not content with the church they had founded, finding it did not have the structure they desired, they moved to Brush Run, Pennsylvania and started *another* church. As their beliefs were moving closer to those of the Baptist Church, they united with the Baptists.

Son Alexander, because of his father, got a position writing in a magazine called *The Christian Baptist*; whereupon he went about condemning creeds, clergymen, church organs, mission societies, seminaries, Sunday schools, Catholicism and anything he considered non-scriptural. Soon they disagreed with the Baptist Church; Thomas and his son Alexander left and formed *Disciples of Christ*. They preached at revivals, inviting believers to leave all organized religions and become part of *his* one *"Christian"* body, with other Christians. Now the funny thing that was happening was that in other parts of the country other self-proclaimed ministers were forming one *"Christian"* body, inviting all Christians to become one under them.

Some united, and those who did not joined in with the Congregational Church. Their *union* had grown in numbers to 100,000, but what did they believe in? They had become so watered down, you could not tell their confederacy of churches from the Universalist church.

What the Campbells originally formed was a loosely knit coalition of independent churches. The *Disciples of Christ* are comprised of three groups:
(1)*The Christian Church (The Disciples of Christ),*

(2)*The Churches of Christ,*

(3)*The Christian Churches* and *Churches of Christ.* Although the original unity of the three denominations created a strong Protestant Church with a potential to be like Main-Line Protestant Religions, soon a schism came about and they were split into groups independently interpreting the New Testament. They reject the Old Testament, insisting on *"No creed but Christ."* This in itself makes them a cult.

Their approach attracts many who do not know their Bible: *"Study your Bible and believe what you want to believe."* They tell Catholics that they can hold onto all they believe and still come to Church of Christ services. Then when they are firmly entrenched, the members of this supposedly non-denominational church begin to attack all the Roman Catholic Doctrines: the *Eucharist* and the other *Sacraments*, the *Blessed Mother*, the *Angels* and the *Saints*, and all the *Treasures of the Church*. The newcomer not knowledgeable of his own faith becomes convinced and is soon attacking his Church and leading other Catholics and Protestants astray.

They are truly dangerous in that they go out of their way to ensnare prospects to their meetings under any subterfuge. They believe that their God-given mandate is to bring new members into their ranks by any means possible. While they consider themselves local good-old-boys, based on the fact that they are a congregational church - just a little bitty church, as an organization - they are one of the largest home-grown non-denominational churches in the United States. Their principal outreach is to minority groups and youth.

1843 - Seventh Day Adventists[15]

The growth of this cult[16] was primarily due to the alleged visions and writings of Ellen White. She had been a student of Henry Miller, a Baptist who predicted the end of the world would come to pass in 1843 or 1844, and formed the Adventists, from which the Seventh Day Adventists emerged. For a more detailed account of the Seventh Day Adventists, see our chapter on them in this book.

1872 - Jehovah Witnesses[17]

One of the most dangerous and aggressive cults, it was founded in 1872 by Charles Taze Russell. His beginnings in the Congregationalist Church, he broke off and started what has become one of the fastest most insidious of the cults, in that it does not tell its victims what the Belief of the Witnesses is. But more about this cult in the chapter on Jehovah's Witnesses.

1879 - Christian Scientist[18]

This cult is not part of the Main-Line Religions and was begun in 1879 by Mrs. Mary Baker Eddy who denies the reality of sin, sickness and death. They do not believe in doctors, hospitals or medicine. More on this cult and its teachings can be found in our chapter on Christian Science.

1889 - Unity School of Christianity[19]

This cult is an outgrowth of *Transcendentalism* (introduced in New England) and another cult - *New Thought*. It was begun by Myrtle and Charles Fillmore who had been suffering from chronic illnesses and crippling debts prior to uncovering what they termed the *transforming philosophy of Unity*. They had studied the concepts and principles of the cults of *New Thoughts* and *Christian Science*. In addition, they took what they considered the best of *Quakerism, Theosophy, Rosicrucianism, Spiritism and Hinduism*. Out of this hodge-podge came a faith belief which cannot be pinpointed as being a copy of anything but a conglomeration of many beliefs. They were able to get followers based on Mrs. Fillmore's testimony. To quote her:

"I am a child of God and therefore I do not inherit sickness."
Another of their beliefs was that *"...whatever man wants, he can have by voicing his desire in the right way into the Universal Mind."*

Some of their other beliefs are:
"God is Principle, Law, Being, Mind, Spirit, All Good, omnipotent, omniscient, unchangeable, Creator, Father, Cause and Source of all that is."

In the Catechism of the Catholic Church, we read:
"God cares for all, from the least things to the great events of the world and its history. The Sacred books powerfully affirm God's absolute sovereignty over the course of events: `Our God is in the Heavens; He does whatever He pleases.' And so it is with Christ, `who opens and no one shall shut, who shuts and no one opens.'"[20]

"God is the sovereign master of His plan. But to carry it out; He also makes use of His creatures' cooperation. This use is not a sign of weakness, but rather a token of Almighty God's greatness and goodness. For God grants His creatures not only their existence, but also the dignity of acting on their own, of being causes and principles for each other, and thus of cooperating in the accomplishment of His Plan."[21]

It would seem that Unity wanted from the outset to appeal to any problem existing in man, and to take care of it by the power of positive thinking. Someone called it a *"religious philosophy with an open end."* It reminds us of the minister who sent out a questionnaire asking people what they like in a Church and then began a denomination to include all the things they liked, and left out all they didn't like.[22] It would be so wonderful if that could be the way it is. But it's not that simple.

Some of the problems that exist with the Unity

philosophy is that they include so many religious beliefs. For instance, Unity students interpret Christian Doctrine and Bible passages as allegorical and mythological, as metaphysical or fantasy, along the lines of Hindu and Transcendental Meditation. They teach that the soul passes through various reincarnations until they all come into Unity.

This *seemingly* harmless cult is the publisher of such inspirational booklets as *Unity, Weekly Unity, Daily Word, and Wee Wisdom*; the best known and most wide-spread is that of *Daily Word*. You may have received and used this booklet in particular, without realizing you were contributing to the promotion and advancement of this cult's philosophy. [I never knew, and I used to read these booklets many years ago, before I began studying the Catholic Church in depth.] You'll very possibly find nine good things in their literature, which you will believe, but the tenth will be complete heresy as far as the Catholic Church teachings go. There's where the confusion lies. *If the nine are right, why is the tenth wrong?*

Like Christian Science, this cult, Unity believes that by thinking good thoughts you can be healed, contending that illness and death have no power over them. One of the differences between them and Christian Science is, they do not charge for their services, but instead proselytize, using testimonies in their periodicals. They have a giant operation subsisting on donations. We have read about cults that use the Radio as their pulpit, others Television and others books and booklets. This cult spreads their thinking on all three. They have a call-in ministry called *Silent Unity* which has a battery of Unity employees answering calls, praying with callers, listening and giving advice.

Their operation has grown to mammoth proportions based on revenue received from grateful donors. Much of their income comes from Catholics and Main-Line

Protestants who are told they can remain in their own churches and belong to this cult. Although this is plainly a misconception, it has worked for Unity!

Think of it. They're not asking you to leave your church, but to take all you have learned from their printed material, audio and videos, for which they solicit you to send money, and pass out the little pamphlets you receive from them to your church community. We need just the opposite to happen. You have to get *Catholic material*, for which you send donations to *Catholic ministries*, which will help them bring out more material. We need you to pass this material out. We need you to evangelize, set up workshops and adult education classroom situations, to offset the proselytizing being done by the cults and sects.

Mid-1800s The New Thoughters

This group of cults was begun by Phineas P. Quimby, a healer from Portland, Maine. He was born in New Hampshire in 1802 and opened an office treating people primarily through hypnosis. He later changed to *healing through the mind*. Quimby gained many patients with his claim that he had healed himself from Tuberculosis.

You will find information on the founder of *New Thought*, "Doctor" Phineas P. Quimby, self-styled doctor and original guru of Mary Baker Eddy, in the chapter on Christian Scientists. Mary was a patient and student of Quimby's on more than one occasion, once for three weeks and once for three months. She also spoke flowingly at his eulogy on the occasion of his death. This relationship was a cause of embarrassment to the members of the Christian Science organization which followed some years later. They played down Mrs. Eddy's involvement with Quimby, and Quimby's involvement with their cult.

He did not believe that Jesus is the Son of God but rather that as with him, Jesus had discovered the mastery of that which he (Quimby) used, that of spiritual healing. Sounds a lot like *New Age* of today, Jesus discovering the God within Himself, just as they say we can find the god within ourselves. *Wild, isn't it?* The Quimby cult never achieved more than local acceptance, although the others, some of whom grew from Quimby's cult, went on to bigger and better things. The beliefs of the *New Thoughters* are basically the same as the Christian Scientists, although there is no connection between the two groups. The New Thoughters believed in God in a pantheistic[24] way.

What do they believe? *New Thoughters* use forms of *Transcendentalism*, *Swedenborgianism*, *mesmerism*, *Hinduism*, and *Spiritualism*. New Thoughters believe in the *divinity of man*. They do not believe in the Trinity - that God is made up of Three Persons in the One God. Although they admire the moral and highly ethical teachings of Jesus, they do not believe in any of the Doctrines left by Jesus and reject the Dogmas of *Original Sin*, the *Trinity*, and the *Atonement of sin*. This conclusively qualifies them as a cult.

Quimby died in 1866, never having founded a church. But soon dissidents from Christian Science began to gravitate to this cult, because it was less stringent than Christian Science in that they could go to doctors or use medicine if they wished (whereas in Christian Science that is forbidden). Unlike Christian Science, New Thoughters do not insist their recruits leave their own churches. But oh what gentle and not-so-gentle persuasion is used after they are in the congregation!

In 1921, one of his followers, Horatio Dresser began to compile and edit the volumes of material Quimby had written. The original manuscript can be found in the Library of Congress. It runs over 2,100 pages. An important find in putting all these writings together was a confirmation of the claims of many New Thoughters that Quimby had developed the theology of Christian Science long before Mary Baker Eddy. This only caused more and more disenchanted Christian Scientists to come over to the New Thought philosophy. Quimby's religion was not as strict as Mary Baker Eddy's. Although they both conformed to the principle of spiritual healing, Quimby's group were allowed to seek help from doctors and medicine if they so chose.

Quimby followers can be found under different names; some are small groups meeting in private homes, rented halls, in small stores with glass fronts, and others are larger denominations: *Church of Divine Science* and the *Church of Religious Science.* There are even affiliated groups of *New Thought* cults. One, the *Affiliated Churches of the Church of Religious Science,* which has over 100 branches or affiliates, are all part of the root planted by Quimby.

All have one thing in common: They do not believe in sickness, the existence of evil, and deprivation or poverty of any sort. Their ideology borders heavily on *Pantheism,* as they do not differentiate between man's power and that of God's. Refusing to believe in the omnipotence of the One God, they believe that *man* is the god of his own destiny - over his body, his wealth, his very existence. They reject the harshness of Calvinism America (Puritans and the like) for a more loving, optimistic belief.

New Thought was made widely known by such authors as Ralph Waldo Trine whose book: *In Tune With the Infinite* sold over one million copies, and by the books of Emmet Fox, a fallen away Catholic who made this cult a household name to thousands of Americans by developing the largest New Thought congregation in New York City by preaching in such places as the Hippodrome and Carnegie Hall.

1934 - Worldwide Church of God[23]

Herbert W. Armstrong was born on an Iowa farm into a family of Quakers. He spent many years in the secular world working in the field of advertising, which he would later use in his future religious efforts. Soon after having married a girl from the Methodist Church, he and his wife ventured to Oregon where they joined a cult. It was in this cult he was first introduced to worshiping the Sabbath on Saturday. He became a minister of this cult and began to preach on a radio station in Eugene, Oregon. From there he moved on to California. He originally founded his cult - the *Worldwide Church of God* as *Radio Church of God* in 1934. Like so many we will be writing about, this church claims that the Church founded by Jesus ended in 69 A.D. and was resurrected in 1934 by him and his ministry!

This cult's teaching is based primarily on *Fundamentalism and Judaism*, as interpreted by Armstrong. It has borrowed from various churches: *Seventh Day Adventists, Mormons, Judaism, Christian Science, Fundamentalism, Jehovah's Witnesses and British-Israelism.*[25] Like the Seventh Day Adventists, members go to services on Saturday and not Sunday. As with the Jehovah's Witnesses they deny our belief in the Trinity and do not acknowledge the Holy Spirit as the Third Person of God. Adopting the traditions of the Jewish people they celebrate the Passover, and following the Old Testament (and the laws of Moses), they observe and practice the Kosher dietary laws set down by him.

Armstrong later promised his followers they would become part of God's family which he *now* claimed included *two Persons*: God the Father and Jesus Christ. Rejecting the Dogma that man has an immortal soul, Armstrong claimed that those who simply follow the laws of the Old and New Testaments will be saved.

To remain in good standing, members of this cult are required to tithe 20% of their earnings yearly to the church and an extra 10% to be given to its charity, every three years. Part of their by-laws is that they are to obey Armstrong without question, observe the seven Old Testament feasts of the Jewish people and spend eight days at summer camp with other members of the cult, each year.

They are forbidden to smoke but may drink alcohol in moderation. They cannot receive medical treatment of any kind. Like Jehovahs, this cult does not observe Christmas, Easter or birthdays. Again like the Jehovahs, they do not vote, join the Armed Services and have little or nothing to do with members of main-stream society.

1970 came and with it, a volcano threatening to erupt and spew out the ashes of division among the members of the cult; they discovered that Armstrong was spending wildly and irresponsibly the congregation's tithing. They found his living in a palatial mansion with an income of $200,000 a year too much to bear, and there was about to be a mass exodus when Armstrong told the members he was stripping his son of all authority, having discovered his son had misused funds indiscriminately. That cooled off things, until the father reinstated the son after he asked for forgiveness. That's when there was another rupture in the wall; members left in protest and began another cult - *Associated Churches of God*. To belong to this new cult, members would not have to tithe up to 30% to be in good standing.

Father and son quarreled again and there was another falling-out and the son formed another cult - *Church of God International*, taking the members with him. And the splinters keep on falling and falling, until....

❊ ❊ ❊

It's alarming to see how all these people began small religious pockets in the Eighteenth and Nineteenth Century, which have in one way or another, on their own, or in conjunction with other harmonious groups of kindred spirits, formed other groups, spreading all over the country. Most of these are of the home-grown variety, having been born in the United States. Brothers and sisters who joined them were crying out for God; and not finding the Spiritual and Ritual in their denominational churches, looked wherever they felt they could find God, in whatever movement which promised them they could have what they had been missing.

Today, many of the smaller groups, like various New Age groups, appeal to an elitist element in our society. Artists, actors, authors, high-level businessmen, financiers, all feel the need to be above the crowd. When someone approaches them on the level of being the chosen, or the intelligentsia, they fall for it. Actually, the smaller the group, as in the case of the Christian Scientists, the more illustrious the members.

We once heard someone say they couldn't convert to Catholicism because they didn't want to go to Church with their servants. They were completely ignorant of what we do at Church. We humble ourselves to the Master. We go to worship, not to be seen. We go to pay homage, not to receive it.

There is such a hunger for God and all that touches the aching heart of man on earth. Don't let the moment go by that you do not reach out to your brother and sister and tell them they *can* find God; He is in our Church and He is waiting for us!

Footnotes

[1]American Family Foundation, Boston, MA - Today's Destructive Cults and Movements, by Father Lawrence J. Gesy, pg.14

[2]*cf*Today's Destructive Cults and Movements, by Father Lawrence J. Gesy, pg.15

[3]You will see this heresy repeated in other cults.

[4]Taken from *Separated Brethren* - William J. Whalen Pg 139, word bolded for emphasis by authors

[5]the Triune God, the Father, the Son and the Holy Spirit, one God in Three Persons, as Christians believe

[6]as they are known, today.

[7]in the 95th Congress

[8]the earth or material world

[9]spiritual world

[10]New Catholic Encyclopedia Vol 13 - Pg. 834

[11]from *Separated Brethren* p.169

[12]The inclination or attraction to evil, arising from the disobedience of Adam and Eve. It specifically refers to desires and inclinations toward bodily and fleshly pleasure. Whereas concupiscence is not evil in itself, it can lead to sin.

[13]not part of the Main-Line religions

[14]A religion founded in the United States

[15]A religion founded in the United States

[16]not part of the Main-Line religions

[17]A religion founded in the United States

[18]A religion founded in the United States

[19]A cult founded in the United States

[20]Catechism of the Catholic Church #303

[21]Catechism of the Catholic Church #306

[22]See chapter on Jehovah's Witnesses

[23]A religion founded in the United States

[24]Pantheism; - is a heresy which began in the garden of Eden, but which was formalized in 1705 by a former Irish Catholic John Toland. Pantheism maintains that God is part of His creation (Immanence). *Catholics* believe that God is present in His creation, but not part of it (Transcendence).

Pantheists believe that there is no personal god.

[25]They teach that the lost tribes of Israel landed in Britain, making the British descendants of the Lost Tribes of Israel.

Anatomy of a Sect

Sects are defined as small groups who have broken away from an established Church. This would apply to most of the sects we will be talking about in this chapter. Traditionally, the small groups which have broken away from the major religions have felt that they needed stronger religious expressions than they were receiving from the larger, established churches.

In the United States, in the late Nineteenth Century and early Twentieth Century, many groups broke away from established churches because of the scourge of Modernism which had infected many mainline churches. Small groups of people felt they had to protect the Bible, the Holy Word of God from those who were degrading it.

Another major cause of breaks between groups and established churches is interpretation of the Bible. This has gotten completely out of hand since John Wycliff and Martin Luther encouraged individual interpretation of Scripture. It has caused rifts which have developed into Cults and Sects. In this chapter, we're going to concentrate on those who kept the main teachings of Christianity, but broke away for their own reasons.

Methods used to talk Catholics into leaving the Church
(1) They invite people to attend the Church;
(2) come to their church's Bible Study;
(3) they're told they can still be Catholic and go to the Catholic Church. Catholics go without understanding.

The final outcome; when they do it is too late.

Many end up leaving the Catholic Church, and others remain, retaining beliefs in opposition to the Church and find themselves confused, often alienated and separated from other Catholics because of the Heresies learned in the sect and they question traditions and devotions that have been part of the Church since the beginning: devotions to Mother Mary, to the Saints, making the Sign of the Cross, to mention a few. They will question the Sacraments using the canned attack: Where is that in Scripture? They will attack the priests, the bishops and even the Pope they once loved.

They do not know that when they leave the Sacraments and the Church they are leaving God. The sect calls the Sacraments evil, and not knowing that one of them is Jesus Himself they are calling evil, leave and try to get others to leave His Church.

Sects and cults as well, cater to people from minority groups, using pastors from their own culture; so many do not know they are leaving the Catholic Church, just that they are with someone who knows them, speaks their language and the method of worship makes them feel a part of the church. This is part of the bad news you must know; the good news is that we can and must evangelize before any more Catholics leave, by not only teaching them the Truth, but by reaching out to them, listening to them, and helping them.

1878 - The Salvation Army

The Salvation Army was started by William Booth in 1865 in the streets of London. He began as an Anglican and then switched to the Methodist Church. The Army most resembles the Methodist Church where he got his background, but rejects the Sacraments that the Methodists kept. They reject Baptism and do not believe in the Lord's Supper; consequently they deny the Eucharist.

The Salvation Army is fashioned after an Army, with a military form of organization. Its founder felt his flock, the inhabitants of the slums, which today would be called "street people" would feel uncomfortable under an organized church atmosphere. So he went into the streets and took his religion with him. It became an army and the founder became the general. He was honored for his work throughout the whole world by royalty and presidents, and died a pauper.

Theologically, the Salvation Army falls into the school of John Wesley's Methodists with a touch of the Holy Spirit. They reject Luther and Calvin's teaching that man has no free will. In their handbook, they state that *"As it is the Salvation Army's firm conviction that these ceremonies are not necessary to salvation nor essential to spiritual progress, we do not observe them."* And so they reject all Sacraments, the seven gifts Jesus left us, at the cost of His Life!

While they have expanded their activities from street people to relief associations, summer camps, hospitals, homes for unwed mothers, nurseries, day care centers and orphanages, they still have their marching band and sing out on street corners. While England is home for this sect, they are very visible in the United States. Two break-offs from the original group, who have formed branches from this sect, are *The American Reserve Workers* and *Volunteers of America*, which were founded by Booth's son and his wife.

1890 - Church of the Nazarene[1]

This sect is the largest of what was originally termed the *"Holiness Churches,"* splinter groups of former Methodists, followers of John Wesley, who sprang up all over the United States between 1890 and 1908. Their *raison d'etre*[2] was to preserve the Wesleyan principles in the Methodist Churches in the United States. Wesley taught that there were two parts to the process of Justification: freedom from sin and the second blessing (being filled by the Holy Spirit). They felt the Methodists were not stressing the holiness aspect of the Methodist persuasion, and so they broke away, forming the Holiness Churches.

The Holiness Churches believe in Christ's Divinity, the Virgin Birth, the Lord's Supper (as a symbolic gesture) and Resurrection of the Body. However, with the Pentecostals, they get into their strong allegiance to the Holy Spirit:

a) Second Blessing, or being filled with the Holy Spirit.

b) An emotional experience in the body as a direct result of this action by the Holy Spirit.

c) Strictly Biblical behavior - inerrancy of the Bible.

They judged that Methodism in the late Nineteenth Century was tainted by compromise with Modernism, a heresy denying the validity of the Bible.[3]

[Modernism; - A Twentieth Century heresy, which had its beginnings in the late Nineteenth Century, it denied everything we believe in. It rebutted Revelation, Scripture and Church Authority. It claimed that Scripture was made up - Jesus never started a Church - He was not Divine - all the Sacraments were bogus. They claimed that St. Paul began the cult of Jesus.]

d) Their main outreach to the faithful is old fashioned revivals. Along with the Pentecostals, it has been most effective bringing in new members to the Holiness Churches.

e) Without making a definite statement to the time, they intimate and indicate that Jesus is coming soon. Every revival meeting has Jesus on His way to the second Coming.

The original *Church of the Nazarene* was founded in Los Angeles, California in 1895. It joined forces with the Holiness churches who joined with an eastern Pentecostal sect, *Association of Pentecostal Churches in America* in Chicago, incorporating the *Pentecostal, Nazarene* and *Holiness Churches* in 1907, under one name *"Pentecostal Church of the Nazarene."* It was joined by the Holiness Church of Christ, a southern group from Pilot Point, Texas in 1908, bringing the number to 10,400 members; now there are over 500,000. In 1919, to distance themselves from the more *radical*[4] Pentecostals (like Jimmy Swaggart, etc.) the Holiness and Nazarene churches dropped the name Pentecostal and became the Church of the Nazarene.

Although remaining loyal in its devotion to the Holy Spirit and the gifts of the Spirit, The Church of the Nazarene, is basically Fundamentalist. You might call them Fundamentalists with tones of Pentecostalism. Their original mission statement read as follows:

They stressed the unity and Trinity of God, the inspiration and sufficiency of Scriptures, the need for redemption because of man's fallen nature, Christ's atonement for our sins, the working of the Holy Spirit in the conversion of sinners, and Luther's old standby, sanctification through Faith alone.

They are conscientious objectors, refusing to take up arms against a brother or sister. They do serve in the military, in noncombatant capacities.

Then, including the beliefs of the Holiness Churches, they added their strong dependence on the working of the Holy Spirit in their lives. The Nazarenes espouse pretty much all that the *Holiness Church* states in their beliefs.

Over the years, especially since the 1960's when the Nazarenes may have hit their fever pitch in terms of Pentecostalism (they were known as holy rollers), the Nazarenes have toned down their services. They have favored a more traditional church service over the Pentecostal, highly emotional tent revivals. That is not to say that the Spirit is not evoked in their services, and that emotions don't run high. But as a whole, they have become much more conservative. They have a strong outreach to bring converts into their ministries. Their favorite target is Catholics, and Hispanics. They opened up a Spanish-speaking mission in Los Angeles at the turn of the century, and have continued their outreach to Mexico, Peru, Africa and other third world countries.

1914 - Assemblies of God

Largest of all the Pentecostal churches in the United States - the Assemblies of God numbers more than 9,000 churches in the United States alone and close to 2,000,000 members in countries around the world. It began in Hot Springs, Arkansas in 1914 and now operates in all 52 States of the union, as well as in more than 75 foreign countries. They have nine Bible Colleges in the United States and 80 colleges world-wide. At last count, there were 884 Missions supported by the Assemblies of God.

It devotes 80% of its proselytizing to Native Americans on Reservations, has *thirteen* missionaries dedicated to the conversion of the Jewish people, fifty ministers to the deaf (or hearing impaired), correspondence courses for prisoners - approximately 400 pastors conduct services in Prisons, an outreach to teen-age gangs.

Their head quarters moved from Arkansas to Springfield, Missouri where they employ 600 men and women, requiring a 3 million dollar payroll. Their main college, *Central Bible College* is located there. Its outreach is through radio, television, printed matter and missionary work. They have a weekly radio program called *"Revivaltime"* which boasts 12 million listeners and is carried by 523 stations. Blacks who were strongly responsible for the initial growth of the Pentecostal movement in the United States have a couple of all black churches till today.

20th Century - Campus Crusaders for Christ, a sect
dedicated to proselytizing Christians on campuses.

As some of you might remember in our personal testimony, we wrote about a boy's detention camp (like a minimum security youth prison) that our family befriended years before our boy ever got in trouble. We felt so blessed. Our children were happy, our daughter was married to a fine young man and they had a beautiful little boy, our grandson. We wanted to put back in the pot - to thank God for all he had given us. *"Whatsoever you do for the least of My children, that you do unto Me. When I was in prison..."* Little did we suspect the devastation that would result from one act of charity.[5]

"One Sunday at Mass, right after Thanksgiving, we saw these young boys come into Church all together. They were obviously not from Malibu. There were Blacks and Mexicans, as well as Caucasian boys. They all looked tough, wore denim prison uniforms, teens anywhere from 15 to 17 years old. I was moved by these young people. No one in the Church community acknowledged their existence. No one exchanged the Sign of Peace with them. They were there, but they weren't there. We went up to them and shook their hands during the Sign of Peace. The boys looked strangely at us. No one had done this before.

"After the Mass, there was coffee and doughnuts in the Parish Hall. The young boys stood off by themselves. We invited them to join us for coffee and doughnuts. We found out they were from a local detention camp in the Malibu mountains, similar to what we used to call Reform Schools in the East. Many were in for drug charges; others had run away from home; some had been thrown out of their homes by their parents. We embraced these children.

"That year, we arranged a Christmas Party for them, got various companies to donate presents and soft drinks, candy and potato chips. Joey Bishop, Burt Lancaster, Al Martino, and a host of musicians performed for the boys, as well as former drug users who had converted to Jesus."[6]

This is how and where we met Campus Crusaders for

Christ. The Camp Director told us that the attention span of these young men was a maximum of twenty minutes, but they were so engrossed in the young men giving their personal testimonies how they had once been on drugs, done time, and then found Jesus, we couldn't distract them even with Ice cream! These Crusaders were not much older than the youth they were speaking to, but they had them mesmerized, captivated by the enthusiasm and love coming from them.

Knowing I had to know about them, I talked my family into going out to Lake Arrowhead. Wandering around their grounds, we met a former Vice President of a large corporation we had done business with. He shared how he had given everything up to serve Christ with the Campus Crusaders. He told us how, each year, he had to go back to his church community and beg for enough money to support him and his family and an equal amount to support the missionary work of Campus Crusaders for Christ.

We attended the seminar that morning, and after the lectures, most of which I couldn't for the life of me understand, we were told to go out and evangelize. They sent us into the poorest barrios. Now, I had never met Mexicans or Mexican-Americans before. I am haunted by the memory of this incident and the harm I could have done. My daughter and I knocked on the first door we came to. (The boys refused to participate in any way. They were smart!) A lovely young woman opened the door. When we explained we wanted to tell her about getting closer to Jesus, she gently told us that she was Catholic, and God forgive us, we said that we were too. I was so stupid, I didn't know that I was proselytizing them to leave the Church. After all we had been told we could stay in our Church and still help bring Jesus to others. I didn't know my own Faith and here I was trying to preach to this young girl. The girl let us in.

Thank God she was the first and the last one we spoke to. They had given us a canned speech to use, something about 4 points. I couldn't tell you then; I cannot for the life of me tell you now what they meant! As I tried to teach her something that had no meaning, I found I couldn't and we went home. That was the end of Campus Crusaders for Christ and me. The Lord protects the foolish, I think; He protected me. But now that I know better, you wouldn't find me dead near this sect or any other sect, no less any other Faith than the one where Christ planted me - the Catholic Church.

I hadn't remembered that since we wrote our book, ten years ago. It was painful recalling the harm I could have done. Maybe it was to let you know how dangerous these sects are, the power that they can wield upon the ignorant (I was ignorant of my Faith) and the impressionable (I wanted to serve Jesus and I was going with the first one who asked me). Is this not what is happening on campuses, today?

Footnotes

[1]A religion founded in the United States

[2]reason for existence - literally reason to be

[3]See chapter on Councils which fought this and other heresies and chapter on Sacraments in Trilogy Book 1 - Treasures of the Church and chapter on Modernism in *Scandal of the Cross and Its Triumph - Heresies throughout the History of the Church*

[4] from the Holiness churches, not the authors' words

[5]Read our testimony *We Came Back to Jesus* which is being updated

[6]from our personal testimony, *We Came Back to Jesus*

Mormonism - Christianity or Cult?

Joseph Smith - Founder of the Mormons

Can money buy souls? Sadly we know that to be true! And if it can, cults like the *Mormons* or *Latter Day Saints*, or whatever new name they use, like *Church of Jesus Christ of Latter Day Saints* are spending hundreds of millions of dollars on secular television in an attempt to bring across the message they are followers of Jesus Christ. **They are no more Christians than any other cult.** They do not declare Jesus God, but only one of many gods; that in itself is enough to eliminate them from belonging to the Body of Christ. This is why it is so important that you know the truth and spread the truth to all Christians. Jesus made a promise that hell would not prevail against His Church. Down through the history of the Church, He has sent powerful men and women through which He would keep His promise. We praise God for again saving His Lambs, by inspiring Mother Angelica to found Eternal Word Television Network where we can get the Truth.

We wonder, sometimes, how we allow strangers and cleverly disguised killers of our souls into our homes! We would not think of opening our doors to someone who could harm our families. I remember how carefully my father and my husband have always guarded their families, painstakenly choosing who they invited into our homes. But now, we often unwittingly invite those advocating totally un-Christian morality into our living rooms. With many T.V. programs, at the beginning, it may not be clear what they are selling, but after awhile it becomes quite obvious.

The really deadly ones are those disguised as lambs. You turn on the television set and you see a lovely scene in a field, children frolicking in the distance, a young couple spreading out a picnic lunch - family! How wonderful, you think to see this on secular television. Then at the end of the *infomercial*, just short enough to wet your appetite, comes the subtle invitation to write or call *The Latter Day Saints of Jesus Christ* for a free copy of the Bible. What they do not tell you is that their Bible was translated to accommodate their four books of Mormon[1] with its *multiple contradictions* of *the Bible*.

Maybe it would be a good idea to keep your dial on EWTN. But a week later, should your remote start cruising the different channels, you more than likely will come upon a very touching scene - grandparents with tiny grandchildren clustered around them, listening attentively to the precious old couple telling stories from the Bible open on their laps. At the end of that touching scene, there is a short message that this had been brought to you by *The Latter Day Saints of Jesus Christ.* What would you think if you did not know better - they're Christians! *They are definitely not Christians.*

Then when you buy periodicals such as the Readers Digest and Time magazine, you will see, sometimes even on the front cover, a great shot of the Mormon Temple with the caption: *The Secrets of America's most prosperous religion.*[2] This magazine, although we are sure the reporter was trying to be objective, presented a principally *subjective* article on Mormonism, based on the new image the Latter Day Saints want to project that Mormons are Christians. **They are not Christians!**

In this chapter, we will attempt to reveal what the Mormons do not tell potential believers, until later on in their conversion; and with some not even then, using the justification they are not mature enough to understand.[3]

With the first book of this Trilogy we are endeavoring to bring you the *Treasures of our Church*, so that should you entertain parting from her loving arms, you depart with a full awareness of Who and what you are leaving. The second book of the Trilogy is on how and why Christian denominations left to begin a new religion. With this the third book of the Trilogy we believe we are called to bring out in the open the teachings of sects and cults, which oppose everything Jesus died for on the Cross. If nothing else, we pray that through these books we can begin to make you aware, in heart and mind, what you, or someone you know are losing, trading in our Church for at best a denomination lacking many of her Gifts, and at worst a sect or cult so devoid of God, you are in danger of losing your immortal soul. Bold? If we do not speak, who will? If we do not cry out, who will hear? Read on, and make your decision to stay and fight, so that our loved ones will know the Truth and live eternally; or leave and lead our loved ones to never-ending death!

How did the Mormons come about?

In 1805, a boy was born to a poor farming family in Sharon, Vermont, and the Smith family named him Joseph. His family belonged to the Presbyterian Church. Another clue to the man that the child would become, is found in his parents who were very superstitious. They believed and depended so completely on illusions and superstition, it was like a creed. It precipitated many lively discussions in their home. Digging came early in Joseph Smith's life, his family obsessively occupied with hunting for buried treasure.[4] They could be seen at different times, often into the wee hours of the morning, shoveling dirt, making deep holes on their property with the hopes of striking it rich. They also made quite a reputation for themselves, telling of visions they were experiencing. *So visions started with his family!*

According to witnesses, the Smith family was not well liked. It was said that the father and his son Joseph showed so little signs of virtue, they could never have believed that Joseph would some day be proclaimed a prophet. On the contrary, they said, what the father and son's conduct revealed was their unrestrained addiction to vice. That Joseph Smith would allege having visions, they had no problem, as this was who he and his family were; but that he would be responsible for the growth of a powerful sect was never in the realm of possibility, as far as they were concerned. Nevertheless they admitted that they had seen strong signs of future leadership. Although Joseph was illiterate, he was very intelligent and innovative. Here again, we see a young man slated for potential greatness, the Lord having given him the gift of leadership; and how he used it, for good or evil, will be determined by the Lord who will judge him and all of us someday.

The family settled in upstate New York; at that time Revival tents were going up one after the other, with people hungering to learn more about the Lord. Joseph Smith leaned toward the Methodist Church, but did not get involved in any denomination. Joseph Smith said that the reading of St. James: *"If there is any one of you who needs wisdom, he must ask of God, Who gives to all freely and ungrudgingly; it will be given to him."*[5] pierced his heart so deeply, he testified, he went out to the woods and prayed. One particular time, after meditating on the passage, trying to grasp its meaning, he said that he was shrouded in darkness. Such a heavy feeling of despair came over him, he felt close to destroying himself. Then a light descended on him. He describes it:

> *"When the light rested upon me, I saw two persons,*
> *whose brightness and glory defy all description,*
> *standing above me in the air. One of them spoke to me,*
> *calling me by name and said, pointing to the other -*
> *This is My Beloved Son. Hear Him!"*[6]

As he believed this was the *Divine* Who was appearing to him; he inquired of the vision, which sect he should join. Whereupon he was told none, as they were all in error, their doctrines blasphemous and their priests dishonest.

For the next three years, Joseph claimed that he had no further contact with the Divine, and that he kept this all to himself, telling no one that the Father and Son had appeared and spoken to him. Then one night,[7] just before retiring, an angel who called himself *Moroni* appeared to Joseph; he told him of a book written on gold plates which contained the history of ancient inhabitants of America, their religion and where they came from. He said the angel told him, as the full Gospel had not been given to the Apostles because they had sinned against God, the Savior came to America and gave these ancient people the full Gospel. The angel allegedly went on to tell Joseph that he had been chosen by God to make known the translation of this book; and to help him, Joseph would find, along with the plates, two *seer stones* called *Urim and Thummim* attached to a breastplate; these would be used to translate the book. Then the angel revealed to Joseph where all this was hidden. But he warned Joseph to tell no one, as the time had as not arrived when the plates were to be revealed.

Ignoring the angel's warning, Joseph said he went to the place where the angel had told him the plates were buried; but just as he was about to lift the plates, the angel Moroni appeared and said that he must wait *four years* before it was time. He then obeyed the angel and returned to this spot once a year. On January 18, 1827, Joseph married Emma Hale without her father's approval.

When four years had passed, the angel Moroni appeared and advised Joseph it was time to retrieve the plates and seer stones. Somehow word got out; Joseph and his wife fled with the plates and seer stones, to her parents' home. The work of translating the books began. A farmer, Martin Harris befriended him and, believing in him and the plates, donated money to Joseph and his wife Emma. Harris became Joseph's secretary, writing down Joseph's translation of the plates (which Harris never saw). There was only one problem - Mrs. Harris did not like Joseph Smith, and so when the first manuscript was finished she burned it. But God[8] saved the day and told Joseph he did not have to translate them again. He had accomplished what he had wanted.

One gone, one year later another comes! Oliver Cowdery was a teacher. When he was staying with Joseph's parents at their farm in New York, he heard of the angel and the gold plates; now he was at Joseph Smith's door, offering his services. He began to write down all that Joseph was translating, and the two quickly became fast friends.

The Story of the Gold Plates

Now, this gets a bit strange, but bear with us; this is what we hear coming from Joseph Smith. Allegedly, the gold plates revealed that there were two ancient Christian tribes living in America - one the *"Jaredites"* whose ancestors left the Tower of Babel in 2250 B.C., settling in Central America,[9] and the second, the *"Israelites,"* who came in 600 B.C. and oppressed the Jaredites. Now Lehi, their leader, (supposedly) divided the *Israelites* into two groups, the good- the *Nephites* who settled in North America and the bad - the *Lamanites* who went to live mainly in South America. According to Smith, God punished the Lamanites and made their skins *dark*; they are the American Indians. The Mormons teach that the American Indians (or Native Americans) - the second tribe of Lehi - are descendants from an ancient Jewish tribe who left Jerusalem around 600 B.C.

The Book of Mormon goes on to say that Mormon and his son Moroni were part of the tribe of the *Nephites* and when a war broke out between the *Nephites* and the *Lamanites*, they were among the few who survived. Mormons believe that the gold plates which Smith used, were inscribed by *Mormon* - an ancient prophet and direct descendant of Lehi. Now Mormon had a son named *Moroni* and during the uprising, Moroni buried the gold plates, and it was he, as a resurrected being, who appeared to Joseph Smith, and revealed their whereabouts.

Smith said that these tribes were all Christians, as Christ had appeared to them shortly after His Ascension and established His Kingdom with them. After His visit the Lamanites and the Nephites lived together for two centuries without incident, holding fast to their belief in Jesus, but then the Lamanites fell into apostasy around 400 A.D.and as a result there was a schism, and this Church, like the one established in Jerusalem, fell.

It is universally agreed among anthropologists that the New World was first occupied by people from *Mongolia*, not from Europe and that they crossed the Bering Strait from Asia to Alaska before the Birth of Christ. Most agree that it had to be between *15,000 and 30,000 years* before Christ, possibly as far back as *100,000 years B.C.* But there is one irrefutable fact; it had to be at least 8,000 years B.C. because the strait of land that had allowed entry into this continent was covered by water and was *not* passable after 8000 B.C. The Book of Mormon puts the arrival of the Jaredite tribe from Mesopotamia at around 2,250 B.C. There is a gap of at least 8000 years, between when the Mormons say the

Jaredites arrived from the Tower of Babel and when anthropologists say the Americas were inhabited by people. So much for that theory which God supposedly gave to Smith, through the gold plates or was it the seer-stone?

There is so much hard evidence against this story, it is hard to believe it, and yet the cult has survived over 170 years.

First, when The Book of Mormon speaks of the Indians being descendants of ancient tribes of Jews, that would mean they would have had to have *spoken one language*, not the more than 2000 languages that were being spoken in the New World when Europeans first landed, with 300 of those languages being spoken in Mexico and Central America, alone. Archaeologists all agree that there has *never* been a time when all the Indians spoke one language. But the Mormons say that they spoke Hebrew!

Second, *their* archaeologists allegedly found *statues*, door lintels, and temple engravings giving rise to the supposition that the Indians had been Jews (Hebrews).
(a) The *statues* blow that theory right out of the water: The statues were of men sporting beards and with hooked-noses suggesting Jewish men, according to the Mormons. They could never have been Jews, as the Jewish people considered statues of men as being craven images and forbidden under Jewish law. (b) Indians do not have beards like the Israelites (Hebrews); they have little or no facial hair.

Now Smith had been thinking about Baptism; so when he *allegedly* came to the place in the plates, where he understood that the Nephites had been baptized for the remission of sins, and as he had not been baptized, he and Cowdery decided to go deep into the woods and ask the Lord about it. As they were deeply engaged in prayer, the story goes that John the Baptist appeared to them. He said that he had been sent by Peter, James and John to confer upon them the Priesthood of Aaron, and later the Priesthood of Melchizedek. Joseph was to be looked upon as the first Elder of the Church, and Cowdery the second Elder. Then, *assumedly*, following John the Baptist's instructions, they went down to the river and first Joseph Smith baptized Oliver Cowdery and then Oliver Cowdery baptized Smith.

In 1829, Joseph and Cowdery went to southern New York and stayed with an old friend of Joseph's, David Whitmer. Here the translations were finally completed. *Now no one outside Joseph Smith ever saw the gold plates!*

When asked, *Joseph's mother* replied she never saw the plates, as Smith said to look upon them meant instant death.

When *his wife Emma* was asked if she had seen the plates, she said she had, but they were covered by a cloth.

Martin Harris was told the same thing: that to look upon the plates was to incur the wrath of God. *So Harris never saw the plates.* He testified that there was a blanket strung across the room separating him from Smith and the *seer stone*, with Joseph Smith on one side translating, and Harris on the *other side* writing down his dictation. But Harris insisted that there was a *seer stone*, and that he believed Smith when he said that words would appear on parchment; Joseph Smith would read them to him and Martin would write them down. This is so confusing! Then according to Martin Harris' testimony Smith was *not* translating but *reading* the English words that God had written on the parchment. Martin said that the plates were not used when he was the scribe. He made no mention of the two *magic* stones *Urim and Thummim*, (the two stones that had been found in the box, along with the plates - none of which Harris saw) which supposedly helped Smith translate the plates. Yet Smith said that he had used the stones for the first 116 pages he had written which Harris' wife had burned. After that, Smith claimed he used the *seer stone* to aid him. *Where are the stones?* The Mormons believe, till today that the magic stones were taken back to Heaven by angels.

Harris said that with the aid of the seer-stone, words would appear, Smith would read them and Harris would write them down. When Smith was finished, he would say "finished" and the words would disappear, and another sentence would appear. But if it was not written correctly, it remained until it was rectified, so that the language was just as it appeared on the alleged gold plates.

According to *Dave Whitmer*, Joseph Smith placed the *seer stone* into a hat, drawing it snugly around his face so no light would come in. Then Smith said that the dark interior would be illuminated by a heavenly light and words would appear on something very much like parchment. The words first appeared in *Reformed Egyptian* and then beneath (the Egyptian words) in English which he would dictate to his scribes.[10]

The highly esteemed Mormon writer Talmadge said *"It is noticeable that we make no reservation respecting the Book of Mormon on the ground of incorrect translation. To do so would be to ignore attested facts as to the bringing forth of that book."*[11]

Now the testimonies of both men are basically the same, eliminating the possibility of any error in the Book of Mormon which supposedly came from the gold plates. But that means that in an effort *"to correct their bible Mormon editors have represented God as an absent-minded semi-literate whose revelation, even regarding His own Son, they have not hesitated to regard as questionable and open to correction."*[12]

Witnesses needed to validate existence of the gold plates

The time came when Smith realized that in order to give credence to his translations, he had to have witnesses who would testify that they exist. He told his three scribes that he had received a message from God that He wanted three witnesses to corroborate the existence of the plates. He took Oliver Cowdery, David Whitmer and Martin Harris out into the woods and allegedly an angel showed them the plates. The three testified to having seen the gold plates. But when the time came that Harris was questioned by an attorney, he admitted that he did not see the plates with his eyes *"as I would that pencil case,"*[13] but with the eyes of faith.

Now, the testimonies given by the three men describing what happened in the woods *differed widely* from what Smith had reported. This caused a problem for Joseph Smith! Smith and his witnesses quarreled and the three left the Church. Smith then told the membership that he had a revelation from God that Harris was wicked. They never recanted their statements. The problem with Joseph Smith and his prophecies, (upon whose authenticity the Mormon faith rests, as well as the veracity of their Prophet Joseph Smith whose words to them are superior to the Bible) is that it was *his scribes*, the very ones who transcribed the words allegedly given to Smith, who gave differing testimonies as to the *existence* of the plates. Now, if his witnesses *had* seen the gold plates, they would have had to believe that Smith was Divinely inspired, and as these plates affirmed the Mormon Church as the true church of God, they could never have left! But they did!

Smith turned on the three, calling them evil and despised by God. If that is so, why would God have chosen them to transcribe His message to Joseph Smith, and why

Brigham Young

had not the Lord revealed to him their wickedness *before* they began this holy work? And if they saw the plates why did their stories conflict with one another? What made them leave? Was it something Smith wanted them to do? Cowdery and Harris are supposed to have returned, but David Whitmer never did. He then declared himself a messenger of God challenging Smith's revelations, calling them false.

When he was losing ground because of the conflicting testimonies of his three divinely chosen scribes, Smith turned to eight new witnesses: four relatives of David Whitmer, the husband of one of the Whitmer witnesses and the last three: Joseph's father, and two brothers. The five Whitmers later recanted their testimonies and left the Smith's church. That left the three who were too close to Smith to be reliable witnesses, but their word is taken as gospel by the Mormons.

Even Prophet Brigham Young, President of the Mormons, on June 5th, 1859, placed doubt on the existence of the gold plates, in a sermon that he gave in the *Morman Tabernacle* in Salt Lake City, Utah:

*"Some of the witnesses of the Book of Mormon, who handled the plates and conversed with the angels of God, were afterwards **left to doubt and disbelieve they had ever seen an angel.** One of the Quorum of twelve - a young man **full of faith** and good works, prayed and the vision of his mind opened and the angel of God*

*came and laid the plates before him, **and he saw and handled them,** and **saw the angel** and **conversed** with him as he would one of his friends; but after all this, **he was left to doubt**, and plunged into apostasy,*[14] *and has continued this work. There are hundreds in a similar condition."*

When a church is founded on the word of a prophet whose revelations are at best questionable, with witnesses after witnesses denying their former testimonies and leaving the church, what foundation does this leave the Mormon church to stand on?

When asked where the gold plates were, Joseph Smith answered his interrogators that an angel had taken them back to Heaven. Now, when we see all the evidence of God's love that He has left on earth, as testimony the Catholic Church and her teachings are true; one example alone, *Miracles of the Eucharist* dating from the 8th century to today, giving ongoing witness that Jesus comes to us *Body, Blood, Soul and Divinity* in the *Real Presence of Jesus in the Eucharist*, then I ask you to ponder why God would take away the only reliable testimony Joseph and his followers had that this ever took place? And if this did not take place, and this is not true, was Joseph Smith of God?

His followers consider Joseph Smith a martyr. Well, there is a real problem with that in that a martyr is one who gives up his life *willingly* for a cause. In the Christian tradition a martyr is one who, rather than apostasize, gives up his life. When Smith had a printing press destroyed that was being operated by Mormons who opposed his teachings on polygamy and multiple gods, they retaliated by coming after him. It is part of Mormon history that Joseph Smith met this angry mob, his six-shooter blazing, exchanging bullets with his enemies, killing two of them and seriously wounding another, before he was shot and killed. Now, there

Joseph Smith was shot and killed by a mob

is no justification for taking a life, any life; but to call this *martyrdom*, is really stretching it. This is not the way that authentic martyrs[15] have reacted to martyrdom, down through the history of our Judaeo-Christian tradition. The early Christians went to their deaths praising God and singing hymns. Like Jesus before him, St. Stephen, the first Christian martyr, died asking God to forgive his persecutors.

Did Joseph Smith have visions?

Now, we would like to believe that Smith *thought* that he had visions. The story of Smith's life makes that at best difficult. But let us suppose Smith *had* visions from God and His Angels. A visit from God, I would think, would tend to make him a *better* man. And in Smith's case, God had chosen him to restore His Church which had failed because of decadent men. Now, forgive me if I am thinking logically but don't you think it is odd that three years after his alleged visions, he is arrested and brought to trial by two neighbors who accused him of being *"an impostor and a disorderly person?"* They said that he was a *"glass-looker"*[16] unscrupulously using a *"peep-stone"* (resembling a crystal ball), to discover where hidden treasure was buried on a neighbor's property. He was found guilty of all charges. Now for over 140 years this had been denied vehemently by first Joseph Smith and then Mormon authorities, until irrefutable evidence was found confirming the trial and its outcome. A *court-cost bill* of the judge in the case, Judge

Albert Neeley, was discovered by a Wesley Walters. Its authenticity has been proven indisputably authentic, and it is now accepted by Mormon historians.

According to court records, in *1826*, he was using a *"peep-stone"* in a hat to find where treasure was buried on his neighbor's property. Now hadn't he said in *1823* that the angel told him *where* the gold plates were and he was not to remove them until four years

One of the alleged visions of Joseph Smith

later in *1827?* If he knew where they were, why was he using a *"peep-stone"* to find them three years after the angel's appearance? Having been visited by God and His angels, how could Smith have used an instrument of the occult, a peep-stone, similar to a crystal ball, whose use was against the law and got him convicted by a court of his peers? Purporting to be Christian, how does Smith's behavior equate with Jesus' words, in reply to the question of obeying the laws of His time, *"Render unto Caesar that which is Caesar's?"* Then I wonder would God have *His* prophet use the above-mentioned peep stone for which he was convicted?

And maybe most important, we come to obedience! Hadn't the angel of God, according to Smith himself, told him *not* to retrieve the gold plates until 1827? I have never heard of God using disobedient messengers. Michael the Archangel *obeyed* God and was victorious over Lucifer who *refused* to obey God. But then again Smith and the Mormons teach that Satan (or Lucifer) was not bad; he was thrown out of heaven because of a *disagreement* between him and Jesus, his *spirit brother*. Again we come to the question, *How could this man - guilty of being disobedient to God's messenger, and a convicted charlatan, have been a prophet chosen by God?* But then *why* so many Mormons? And why such growth? Do they know their own history?

Talking of history, Smith said that his spiritual experiences, his visions and visitations by God and His angels caused such a stir, such an excitement, it brought him much suffering and persecution. But in checking records, there is nothing mentioning his alleged visions, nor his Divine visits, nor his notoriety, nor his persecution. Isn't that strange? Even at this time, let someone say that an oil spot appears to be an Angel or the Virgin Mary, it is on television or at least in the papers. But here, nothing. Strange!

Another curious fact is that during the 1830s, nothing regarding such an important occurrence, as Smith's visions, appeared in Mormon, non-Mormon, or other publications. Then couple that with few Mormons *knowing* anything about it. Since the vision is of crucial importance to the Mormon Church, the very foundation upon which the existence of the Mormon Church stands till today, it is indeed strange and makes one wonder!

In 1853, Joseph's mother wrote her own history of the beginning of the Mormon Church and how it came about. But it read suspiciously like her son's book, as she was using *his history* of the Mormon Church as her reference of his first vision. Her earlier handwritten version had no mention of his vision! Wouldn't you think that since it had gotten such acclaim and widespread notice, she would have written about this right in the beginning, before she wrote about anything else?

Let us talk about Smith's first vision: Joseph Smith wrote *three* handwritten renderings of what happened during that first vision with *major, critical inconsistencie*s:

In one version, he wrote that only *one Person* appeared to him - the Lord, and Joseph said that he was sixteen years old at the time.

In another, he said that *angels* appeared, and he was *fourteen* years old.

And then, in the third memoir, he said *two Persons* visited him, *the Father and the Son.*[17]

Now, it's understandable that there may be little haziness on unimportant details of an occurrence, but when you cannot decide if there was one Person-the Lord, or two angels, or the Father and the Son Who made an appearance and gave you the word to restore His Church, I think we have a problem!

Now if that does not boggle your mind, Smith helped Cowdery (one of his scribes and the Mormon Church's first historian), to write a history of the Church's beginnings; it includes all the circumstances surrounding the vision but *it does not include the Father and the Son Appearing to Joseph Smith.* What he wrote instead was that Joseph went into the woods to pray and find out if God really existed. Then a messenger appeared to Joseph and told him his sins were forgiven. Now what happened? Joseph first wrote of One Person, then two angels, then the Father and the Son, three different versions of one vision. Now he is assisting his first historian and there is a completely different version altogether, with now Joseph going into the woods and an angel appearing to him telling him God forgave him. With something so monumental, how could Smith allow Cowdery to make such an error recounting his vision in the woods?

If you recall, Joseph Smith said that there was a great

religious revival going on in his hometown in the spring of 1820; yet scholars have found no record of a revival in Palmyra, New York that year. If that is not evidence that something is wrong, neither could *Mormon* researchers find any verification of Smith's testimony regarding the vision!

Joseph Smith - Prophet or Pretender?

A true Prophet and his prophecies must agree with God's revelations coming to us through the Old and New Testaments. Jesus said that He did not come to abolish the Law (referring to the ancient teachings of the Jews) but to fulfill it. St. Paul, Jesus' Apostle, cautions Christians, in his letter to the Galatians:

*"....there are some who trouble you and want to pervert the gospel of Christ. But even if we, or an Angel from Heaven, should preach to you a gospel contrary to that which we preached to you, let him be anathema (*cursed*). As we have said before, so now I say again, If any one is preaching to you a gospel contrary to that which you received, let him be anathema."*[18]

Now, Joseph Smith not only went against the teachings of the Old Testament but he attacked the New Testament, as well when he taught that:

(a) there are many gods made up of flesh and bone;[19]

(b) polygamy - the taking of multiple wives[20]

(c) and the pre-existence of souls.[21]

Ask the two young men who come to your door promoting Mormonism as Christian, how they can make that statement when their teachings are so contrary to that which the Lord passed down to His children through His Word. You will find that if you challenge them, they cannot answer you, but instead using a canned speech, they go on with their rote delivery.

Joseph Smith made prophecies after prophecies that never came to pass:

(a) In 1835, he predicted, a huge gathering of Mormons would assemble in front of a new grand temple in Western Missouri. The assemblage never happened nor was there a temple for them to gather in front of.

(b) Next our prophet prophesied, seeing the conditions of the times, that there would be a Civil War, and the Mormons use this to verify Joseph Smith as a prophet and their cult as legitimate till today; but they fail to mention that along with that, he prophesied that Great Britain and other nations would join in and there would be a great famine and destruction. Sorry, don't want to burst your balloon, but that never came to pass!

(c) Joseph Smith prophesied the end of the world and Jesus' Second Coming in 1835, and as far as we can see that never happened, either.

Sadly, he credited God for all these predictions. Now, doesn't God get blamed for enough happenings, without some false ones being thrown in? Our dear Mormon friends, good people that they are, believe that Smith was a prophet, and they base all they live and believe in, on that premise. But Joseph is not the last prophet from God because Holy Scripture tells us that Jesus is the *last.*

"In times past, God spoke in partial and various ways to our ancestors the prophets; in these last days, He spoke to us through His Son, Whom He made heir of all things and through Whom He created the universe."[22]

Is the Book of Mormon equal to the Bible?

Speaking of literary worth, there are so many serious problems with the Book of Mormon, it cannot fail to lead the reader to genuine *doubts* that it is comparable, no less equal to the Bible, as Mormons claim. First off, we must say, speaking as authors, that the Word of God is so pure, so clearly written, so touchable, so understandable, so followable, it is a Book for everyone at every time in their lives. There is so much contained in every sentence, you could write a book on each and every thought and happening in the Bible. In contrast, scholars who have struggled through the Book of Mormon will tell you it is boring and very difficult to get through. But, in addition some serious theological and historical discrepancies that are disturbing are:

Close to ten percent of the Book of Mormon is almost *word for word*, along with some direct quotations, from the unrevised version of the *King James Bible.* And this from a Book supposedly coming from gold plates inscribed and buried by Moroni in Palmyra, New York in *425 A.D.,* 1186 years before the original King James version of the Bible was printed? Does it seem plausible that the Book of Mormon would have passages written in the same style as the original King James version of the Bible? You may notice that there is a difference between the phraseology of Bibles, depending on the period they were translated into the vernacular.

The only feasible conclusion any right thinking, logical person can come to is that this Book of Mormon, is not of an ancient people through whom God has chosen to speak to His people, but a modern day plagiarism of the King James Bible of the *17th Century,* (containing errors that have since been corrected). One change which glaringly stands out is: In the King James version of the Bible written in 1881, the doxology, *"For thine is the kingdom, and the power, and the glory, for ever"* is included at the end of the Lord's Prayer; it is no longer present in the *revised* King James version of the Bible, as it lacks authenticity.[23]

Hurry up Mormon scholars and change the Book again!

Although the Mormons allege that the Book of Mormon is unchanged since it was first dictated by Joseph

Smith, there have been more than 2000 corrections, not only of mis-spellings and awkward grammar, but of text and content, with some words and phrases added, and others omitted.

Some changes more crucial than others is the change of names: *The original name of King Mosiah had been Benjamin.* Are Mormons suggesting that God had a lapse of memory when He had originally given Smith the name Benjamin? Please fellas, God is perfect no matter how long you preach he is being perfected.

When Smith is not quoting the King James Bible, and he is on his own, he makes blatant errors in theology, errors that our perfect God would never make (Smith claims God gave him these translations). For example:

(a) There is *proof positive* that cows, oxen, asses, and horses did not exist at the time the Nephites assumedly arrived here, as the Book of Mormon teaches;

(b) The use of a mariner's compass did not exist at that time;

(c) In The Book of Mormon, it says that Jesus would be born in Jerusalem; whereas we all know that Jesus was born in Bethlehem [a blatant contradiction or at best error].

(d) In the Old Testament, in Jacob, God tells us that polygamy was abominable in the sight of God.[24] But we find that in the Book of Mormon God commands it to be practiced and says it is righteous.

They are going after Indians, Mexicans, Hispanics from Central and South America using warped, unauthenticated archaeology. For example:

They are descendants of the original tribes of Jews who came to this continent and to whom Jesus gave His Church. As we gave the infeasibility of this, to add to that in Mexico alone (as we have seen many times, when the Indians from all parts of Mexico come to visit their Lady of

Guadalupe on her feast day), there many different languages with many different skin colors, with many different features, some tall and some short in stature, many beautiful languages flowing smoothly from their tongues. This evidence alone disputes the Book of Mormon with their concept of the origin of the people of the New World, along with the gold plates upon which the whole Mormon Church stands. Mormon apologists are having a hard time trying to wiggle out of a tight spot. Not even they can explain the obvious discrepancies and inconsistencies exposed by the very anthropologists and archaeologists trying to justify Joseph Smith's prophetic words that only two groups of ancient people inhabited this continent, the Jaredites and the Israelites.

So much for the Indians having been ancient Jews from whom the Book of Mormon originated. But what a devious tool to use on unknowing people starving for something to make them proud of who they are. Why have they not been told that they are children of the Father, the King of the Universe and they are so important to Him, He sacrificed His only begotten Son Jesus for them? Why have they not been told that when Jesus was incarnated, they became part of His Family, and that Jesus loves them so, He left them the Queen of Heaven and Earth as their own Mother? It doesn't get better than that!

We could go on and on, but it has been done so much better and so thoroughly in the books where we got much of our research, we will leave this now.[25] We just want to say do not be deluded. There is no sound archaeological authentication for the preposterous proposals made by the Mormons to draw Christians away from Christ. Remember they say that they believe Jesus is god with a small "g," not God the Second Person of the Holy Trinity, as all Christians believe. **They are not Christians!**

What do Mormons believe? *Ask yourself if you would trade **the Way and the Truth and the Life Who is Jesus** for this!*

"Mormonism's Strange Doctrines
        The doctrines of Mormonism grew stranger as the cult developed. Presently, Mormon doctrines are as follows: [Note: These doctrines are documented
from Mormon writers, not anti-mormon writers.]
1. The true gospel was lost from the earth. Mormonism is its restoration. They teach there was an apostasy and the true Church ceased to exist on earth.[26]
2. We need prophets today, the same as in the Old Testament.[27]
3. The book of Mormon is more correct than the Bible.[28]
4. There is no salvation outside the church of Jesus Christ of Latter-day Saints.[29]
5. There are many gods.[30]
6. There is a mother god.[31]
7. God used to be a man on another planet.[32]
8. After you become a good Mormon, you have the potential of becoming a god. [33]
9. God the Father had a Father.[34] One of the purposes of the Seer was "to elucidate" Mormon Doctrine.[35]
10. God the Father has a body of flesh and bones.[36]
11. God is in the form of a man.[37]
12. God is married to his goddess wife and has spirit babies.[38]
13. We were first begotten as spirit babies in heaven and then born naturally on earth.[39]
14. The first spirit to be born in heaven was Jesus.[40]
15. The Devil was born as a spirit after Jesus, *"in the morning of pre-existence."*[41]
16. Jesus and Satan are spirit brothers.[42]
17. A plan of salvation was needed for the people of earth so Jesus offered a plan to the Father and Satan offered a

plan to the Father but Jesus' plan was accepted. In effect the Devil wanted to be the Savior of all Mankind and to *"deny men their agency and to dethrone god."* [43]

18. God had sexual relations with Mary to make the body of Jesus. [44]

19. Jesus' sacrifice was not able to cleanse us from all our sins. [45]

20. Good works are necessary for salvation. [46]

21. There is no salvation without accepting Joseph Smith as a prophet of God. [47]

22. Baptism for the dead. [48] This is a practice of baptizing each other in place of non-Mormons who are now dead. Their belief is that in the afterlife, the *"newly baptized"* person will be able to enter into a higher level of Mormon heaven.

23. There are three levels of heaven: telestial, terrestrial, and celestial." [49, 50]

With all we have uncovered, is there any doubt that there is reason to question whether Joseph Smith is a Prophet? And if he is not a Prophet but a Pretender, then is the Book of Mormon, upon which this cult stands, authentic? Is there any doubt in your minds that Mormons are not Christian? Read more about this dangerous cult. [51] Jesus said *"Whoever is not with Me is against Me."* [52]

As we were rounding up this chapter, we came across this article we had written seven years ago for our newspaper. [53]

Battle of the ISMS; Mormonism
"Whom shall I send?"

This is not an outcry against any Sect or Following of any of our brothers or sisters. It is an appeal by *Christ* to His Children. Who will spread *His* Word?

This is The *Good* Newsletter. It has been so difficult to write this column on Mormonism. We, here at the

Community, have prayed and prayed. We now ask the Holy Spirit to direct our words that they might instruct you as He would have you instructed. With so many of our young people being wooed into Cults and Sects that threaten our Church and are contrary to the true teachings of Jesus, we felt impelled to share with you some of the dangers our country and world is facing.

A very holy priest pointed out our need to recognize that there are two banners, that of Jesus and that of Satan. It is essential that we know the difference! Now, more than ever it is crucial for us to learn our Faith which has been passed down to us these 2000 years through the Roman Catholic Church that was founded by Jesus Himself. Jesus did not allow Satan to tempt Him because Satan had no authority over Him. We should be prudent in questioning the authority of those who would proselytize to *us*. Although *we* will not accept false teachings, we must be aware of that which is being fed to our *family members*.

Many of us have not been concerned by the growing numbers of Mormonism as we have thought of it as another of the Protestant denominations. But they themselves will vehemently deny it.

[They have taken a new tact: Their new *public relations* approach is to *de-emphasize* that which is controversial in their Book of Mormon, in an attempt to draw Christians away from their Churches, by *appearing* Christian. What cults do is they draw you in with the Name of Jesus, but once inside the cult, the Name Jesus and His teachings are slowly changed to the Guru of the cult, in the instance of the Mormons, it is Joseph Smith and his philosophy.]

The Church of Latter Day Saints or Mormons has a belief uniquely its own, separate from any of the Truths we Christians hold dear. For example, like something very closely smacking of the new-old heresy now called New Age, Mormons believe that *God was once man who evolved into God*, that He had a body and was married and procreated billions of spirit children. They teach God had a father and other ancestors on other planets. To quote the Mormons' favorite teaching, *"As man is, God once was. As God is, man may become."*

If that does not shock you, how does this make you feel? They also believe that Jesus and Lucifer were both spirit children of this God, but Lucifer rebelled. Jesus took on Human Form and became Savior while His *brother* Lucifer talked one third of the brothers and sisters to follow him and they became *demons*. They claim that Jesus, after His Resurrection, came to this hemisphere and appointed another twelve Apostles. They further preach that the church in Jerusalem and the church in America became apostate and lost all authority to preach or baptize.

They contend that every human being has lived *before* (Reincarnation?) with a heavenly father, but has agreed to undergo the test of mortality. They further preach that we are born *without* sin, that through ritual observances and good works we can pave our way to becoming *gods!* They believe if a man is baptized a Mormon and marries a Mormon woman in the Mormon temple, observes all the dietary laws, tithes, obeys Mormon priests and leads an upright life *he will become a god of his own planet*; he and his wife will procreate spirit children who will worship them as *gods!*

There are very noticeable parallels between Mormonism and Islam (Moslems). Moslems and Mormons have adapted the Old and New Testaments *to their own scriptures* [with their own translations]. Although they both revere Abraham, Moses and Jesus, they ascertain that another prophet was given God's *final revelation* to mankind. For Moslems, it is Mohammed and for Mormons, Joseph Smith Jr. They both

Mormon Temple in Salt Lake City, Utah

encouraged polygamy and enforced strict dietary laws.

Whereas we Catholics and Protestants, are very often practicing birth control - having the ideal American family of a boy for you and a girl for me, Mormons have a *high* birth rate and a *low* death rate. When you couple that with their aggressive missionary work, you have one of the fastest growing major cults in our country. Mormons number 4.1 million in this country with 2.5 million in foreign countries.[54] Whereas less than half of our Jewish brothers and sisters belong to a Temple and barely 13 percent claim to attend any kind of service regularly, two out of every three Mormons are *actively* engaged in learning their beliefs and *spreading* them. Our mainline Christian denominations, with their numbers shrinking, are not faring much better than their Jewish brothers and sisters.

Most of the Mormon concentration had been in the Rocky Mountain and Western states, but now with their 35,000 missionaries going door-to-door, skillfully persuading families to leave their churches, they have spread throughout our 50 states, with swelling numbers of converts in Texas, Florida, Virginia, and Hawaii. Souls not knowing their own faith, have believed the Mormon missionaries who have told them that their Churches are *apostate and corrupt*, and have left their Churches.

There are now seven times as many Mormons worldwide than there were prior to World War II. Young Mormons in their late teens or early 20's consider it an honor to go out and preach, working 16 hours a day 6 days a week. They hold off furthering their educations, marrying and pursuing careers until a 2 year assignment is completed; their parents financing them up to and in excess of $400 per month. The Mormon missionary program far exceeds any of the other churches in America with the largest Protestant religion, the

Southern Baptists sharply trailing behind with 3800 missionaries.[55]

* * *

The Mormons used to come to visit us quite regularly when we first moved into our house in Westlake Village, California. One Thanksgiving morning, we were home. We saw two young men approaching the house, dressed in black. We weren't sure if they were Mormons or Jehovah's Witnesses at first.

This was the typical *young one-old one* setup. One was the teacher; one was the student. The student was wide-eyed, as if this was all new to him. Bob looked at them as they walked up the steps to our front door. He had such compassion for them. Here they were on Thanksgiving Day, out trying to bring people to God. Wow! *"Let's invite them in,"* he said, *"and share about Jesus."*

Obviously, Bob didn't know anything about Mormons. As they approached our front door, they could see we had a series of six tiles showing Our Lady of Fatima with the three children. We had bought this in Fatima, and put it up some years before. That made them a little nervous. But they could see that our garage was a disaster, boxes all over the place [They did not know we were manufacturer's representatives in the gift field, and kept our samples in the garage]. So when they rang the bell, we answered, smiling with the love of Jesus. They asked:

"Did you folks just move in?" hoping that the tile of Our Lady of Fatima was not ours, but the previous owners.'

"No," we answered, "we've been here for five years." Their faces sunk, but not as much as when we fully opened the door to our home. They could see a full view of our living room, which has been described by the pastor of our Church as Vatican West. Msgr. Tom O'Connell would tell us:

"You've got more statues and religious paintings in your house than we have in the church." To which we would reply, "and your point is???"

But for these poor Mormons, to see all that and our two smiling *"with the love of Jesus"* faces staring at them, they must have wished they could have passed us by that morning.

We invited them in; they refused, content to stand at the doorway. They weren't getting into that trap. Once in, they were afraid we'd turn them into card-carrying Catholics. They began their pitch, or at least the older one did. The young one just stared at us as if we were from another planet. We told them we were Catholics. The teacher responded with the normal cultist response, *"My parents were Catholics, until we learned the truth."*

Then they asked if they could leave us some material, in particular the Book of Mormon. Bob was so innocent. "Sure," he said, "but wait a minute. I have some things I'd like to leave with you." With that, he ran into the library and got some little books we had just purchased from the Blue Army. One of them was *"Mary faces her Accusers."*

He handed it to the leader. "If you read this book, I'll read your book of Mormon." The leader backed away from the book as if it was poison. "No, I couldn't do that. I wouldn't have time to read it."

Bob responded, a little hurt, "Oh, then I won't have time to read your book."

They prepared to leave, knowing this had not been a good call. Penny and Bob, hand in hand, said to them: "We think what you're doing is really wonderful, coming out like this on Thanksgiving Day. We really love you."

This was more than the older one could handle. He wanted out of our doorway. He nudged his protégé on. But the younger man couldn't believe what we had said. He looked at Penny. "Do you mean that? Do you really love us?" She answered yes, and as they were walking away, the younger one kept looking back. We knew the older one was going to have to do a lot of explaining about us. We did not fit into the mold he had manufactured.

✳ ✳ ✳

But that was not our last experience with the Mormons. We met up with another group of them in, *you'll never believe it*, Siena, Italy. We were traveling with our family, just the four of us in a car, driving all over Italy visiting the shrines. Typically, once we entered a town, especially a large city, we would get lost trying to find the shrine, so we would begin asking.

Well, this time, we had asked and asked and asked, and were getting more and more lost. As we passed the train station, we saw two young men on bicycles. They were dressed in black pants, white shirt and black ties. We couldn't believe it. They looked just like the Mormon young men we had seen back in the United States. As we got closer to them, we saw the name tags they wore. Sure enough, they were Mormons.

We approached them, not so much to get instructions on how to get to the shrine of St. Catherine of Siena, as to ask what they were doing in Siena. We got both answers. They had us follow them to where we would find directions to the Church of St. Catherine, and at the same time, told us their story.

They were from the United States. They spend two years in evangelization (we call it proselytizing) which is paid for by their folks. They are given a six-week training course in the language and customs of whatever country they're going to be working in, and then they're sent overseas. In this instance, the Mormon Church had an apartment in Padua. These young men would go there and wait, practicing their language skills. When they were called, they would go to whatever city they were assigned, and begin door-to-door, trying to sell Mormonism to the Italians.

We thought to ourselves, "Fat chance they've got, getting the Italians to convert. You cut an Italian, and he bleeds Catholic." But to our amazement, they said they were getting some people to listen to them, even though they spoke chicken-Italian.[56] We don't know if they were sincere or if they just wanted us to think they were making progress. But it did frighten us. We thought they were just in the United States, but Italy? Since we began bringing pilgrimages to Mexico, we find that the Mormons have made tremendous headway in Mexico, especially with those who would rather think of themselves as Indians than Spaniards. It all stems from Joseph Smith's story that Jesus came to the Indians in the United States.

✲ ✲ ✲

Because of its enormous wealth, their estimated net worth of $8 billion far exceeds the assets of the *Vatican*, an estimated yearly income of $2 billion, (75% coming from Mormons tithing) and power (holdings in some of our most influential and largest of corporations,) their use of millions ($12 million in Reader's Digest alone) for ad campaigns and clever television spots, the Mormon church is rapidly and dangerously escalating.

The Mormons believe that the end is at hand. Well, be that as it may, we believe that the lines are being clearly drawn. We are, as possibly never before, in the times that Jesus spoke of where we are either for Him or against Him. *Which banner will you follow? Will it be that of Jesus and the Cross!*

Footnotes

[1]whose teachings they hold superior to the Bible

[2]on the front cover of Time magazine August 4, 1997

[3]Down through the centuries heretics, schismatics and cultists have kept the truth from the faithful with that demeaning judgment. Well we *do understand* - just tell us the truth!

[4]Sixty-two people who knew the family bore witness to this, and signed their names attesting to the authenticity of their testimony. - from *Mormonism Unveiled* by E.A. Howe.

[5]Jas 1:5

[6]*Mormonism, The Prophet, the Book & the Cult,* Peter Bartley

[7]September, 1823

[8]according to Smith

[9]You hear a lot of this unfounded archaeology pridefully repeated by new Hispanic converts to Mormonism in Mexico and Central America because of Mormon missionaries using this to proselytize them.

[10]according to David Whitmer's *Address to All Believers.*

[11]*The Vitality of Mormonism,* cited in A.A. Hoekema, *The Four Major Cults* pg.18 - *Mormonism, the Prophet, the Book and the Cult,* Peter Bartley

[12]*Mormonism, the Prophet, the Book and the Cult,* Peter Bartley

[13]Harris - *The Confusion of Tongues* by Charles Ferguson

[14]apostasy - the complete repudiation of the faith of a church, in this case the Mormon Church

[15]Read more about Martyrs in Bob & Penny's book: *Martyrs, They died for Christ.*

[16]another word for a fortune teller

[17]from the Tanners - *Mormonism, Shadow or Reality?*

[18]Gal 1:7-9

[19]still Mormon theology

[20]no longer practiced by the Mormon Church after polygamy was outlawed in the United States

[21]still Mormon theology

[22]Hebrews 1:1

[23]*cf Mormonism, the Prophet, the Book and the Cult,* Peter Bradley

[24]Jacob 2:23-27

[25]See Bibliography for great books to learn more conclusively about Mormonism.

[26]*Mormon Doctrine, by Bruce R. McConkie, pg. 635*

[27]*Mormon Doctrine, pg. 606*

[28]*History of the Church, 4:461*

[29]*Mormon Doctrine, pg. 670*

[30]*Mormon Doctrine, pg. 163*

[31]Articles of Faith, by *James Talmadge, pg. 443*

[32]*Mormon Doctrine, pg. 321*

[33]*Teachings of the Prophet Joseph Smith, pgs 345-347, 354*

[34]*Orson Pratt in The Seer, page 132*

[35]*The Seer, page 1, 1854*

[36]*Doctrine and Covenants, 130:22*

[37]*Joseph Smith, Journal of Discourses, Vol. 6, page 3.*

[38]*Mormon Doctrine pg. 516*

[39]*Journal of Discourse, Vol. 4, p. 218*

[40]*Mormon Doctrine, page 129.*

[41]*Mormon Doctrine, page 192*

[42]*Mormon Doctrine, pg. 163*

[43]*Mormon Doctrine, pg.193; Journal of Discourses, vol. 6, p.8*

[44]*Journal of Discourses, Vol. 4, p. 218, 1857*

[45]*Journal of Discourses, Vol. 3, p. 247, 1856*

[46]*Articles of Faith, pg. 92*

[47]*Doctrines of Salvation, Vol. 1, pg. 188*

[48]*Doctrines of Salvation, Vol. II, pg. 141*

[49]*Mormon Doctrine, pg. 348*

[50]"Basic Christian Doctrine" by Matthew Slick, www.carm.org/basicdoc.htm.

[51]Read in more detail from the great books and E-Mail from which we obtained much of our research in our Bibliography.

[52]Mt 12:30, Lk 11:23

[53]The Good Newsletter

[54]That was based on 1989-90 figures. It has escalated greatly since then

[55]again, these are 1989-90 figures.

[56]That means poor Italian

Jehovah's Witnesses

A Media Blitz for Souls

Every piece of material we've read about Jehovah's Witnesses begins in the same way. They talk about the door-to-door *"ministers"* of the Witnesses as *cute, harmless people, completely dedicated,* who will not let you live until they have an opportunity to leave you some Watchtower material and come back for a second go-round.

They come out every day of the year, be it Thanksgiving (which they don't celebrate), Christmas (another holiday not honored by the Witnesses), a boiling hot day in the middle of the summer. Everybody knows about them; everybody has been exposed to them. They're sort of like the Fuller Brush man that used to come around. You knew you were going to be accosted by one of them at some time in your life.

But that's only the first paragraph, the introduction to the Jehovah's Witnesses. The war stories about the actual ordeals with Jehovah's Witnesses can be *bloodcurdling.* Digging deeper into these accounts of experiences with the Jehovahs, we find that disarming quality they have when they first encounter people at the door of their home changes drastically once they get inside. They become very aggressive in lambasting whatever Faith you happen to believe in, and promote King Jehovah's way.

They use Scripture a lot. I shouldn't capitalize it when using it in the same sentence as Jehovah's Witnesses, because they have desecrated the Word of God so badly it's not really recognizable as having come from the Bible. But like many of their cult counterparts, they use anything they can, as long as it can be twisted to meet their agenda. They have rewritten the Bible. Originally, they used the King James Version, but only those areas which did not conflict with Jehovah's Witnesses theology.

In the 50's, however, they wrote their own Bible, which is called *New World Translations of Holy Scripture*. This is the Jehovah's Witnesses version of the Bible, in which hundreds of changes were made, and anything that does not agree with their theology is thrown out. We invite your attention to what is written by St. John with regard to playing games with Scripture at the end of the Book of Revelation:

"I warn everyone who hears the prophetic words
in this book:
If anyone adds to them, God will add to him
the plagues described in this book,
and if anyone takes away
from the words in this prophetic book,
God will take away his share in the tree of life
and in the holy city described in this book."[1]

Jehovah's Witnesses fit very neatly in the definition we gave at the beginning of the book on Cults:

"A destructive cult or sect is a highly manipulative group which exploits and sometimes physically and/or psychologically damages members and recruits.

A destructive cult:

> **a)**dictates, sometimes in great detail, how members should think, feel and act;
> **b)**claims a special exalted status (i.e. occult powers: a mission to save humanity) for itself and/or its leaders - which usually sets it in opposition to mainline society and/or the family;
> **c)**exploits its members psychologically, financially, and/or physically;
> **d)**utilizes manipulative or *"mind control"* techniques, especially for the denigration of independent critical thinking, to recruit prospects

and make members loyal, obedient, and subservient; and

e)causes considerable psychological harm to many of its members or to its members' families."[2]

When you open your door to three seemingly harmless women, invite them into your home and possibly your head, without knowing their game plan, are you aware that this casual morning or afternoon visit may expose you to more than you bargained for? Are you ready for possible ruination; spiritually, financially, and mentally, with the possibility that your children, exposed to cults like this, could possibly run off and join them, never to be seen again?

Jehovah's Witnesses as an organization controls one of the largest worldwide print and media complexes, with printing factories in many countries from which over a hundred million copies of Witness material is pumped out each year. Now don't think for a moment that this is being printed and then dumped into a garbage can just so they can boast having these figures. No! This is being distributed to brothers and sisters all over the world. One of their books, *"The Truth that Leads to Eternal Life"* has over 80,000,000 copies in print. We're told that it is the fourth all-time best seller. The only books that top it are: 1) *The Bible*, 2) *Quotations from Chairman Mao*, 3) Noah Webster's *American Spelling Book*.

In 1958, *The Divine Will International Assembly of Jehovah's Witnesses* at New York's Yankee Stadium and New York's Polo Grounds (since demolished) shared an attendance of 253,922. And that was forty years ago, my friends. In 1974, they had an attendance of 4,925,643 at their annual communion, and in 1985, the number swelled to 7,792,109. That's scary, folks.

There are so many things we want to tell you about

Assembly of Jehovah's Witnesses at Yankee Stadium in 1958

the Jehovah's Witnesses that we don't know where to start. But you should know a short history of who they are and how they got there.

✻✻✻

Charles Taze Russell
Founder and first guru

Born in Pittsburgh in 1852, he was the son of a haberdasher. He began his religious training as a Congregationalist, but his study of the Bible led him to deny the existence of hell, the doctrine of the Trinity and to express Arian views denying the Divinity of Jesus Christ.

[Author's Note: *For this we can thank John Wycliff who first came up with the concept of each man interpreting Scripture for himself, and good old Martin Luther who really rammed it home in his 95 Theses against the Catholic Church. The evil that men do lives on after them. Would that make a book.]*

Assuming the title of "Pastor" he left his haberdashery and began to organize Bible Study groups. We have to ask ourselves why? What was his training? What gave him the idea that he was qualified to interpret Scripture, number one, and to teach it to people number two? And why did people listen to him, number three?

If we were to do a listing of the founders of the cults we're writing about in this book, and give you their credentials, you would have to wonder how their followers are still with these cults or ever joined them in the first place.

This haberdasher who never finished high school becomes a pastor. The foundress of the Seventh Day Adventists had a third grade education and was struck by a rock as a child, which affected her for the rest of her life! Mary Baker Eddy, foundress of the Christian Scientists, had a limited formal education. Joseph Smith, founder of the Mormons, who based his new religion on gold plates that no one saw but him. We're not trying to be critical of these

Charles Taze Russell

people, but dear Lord, how can anyone take them seriously? How can people give up their lives based on the theology of these people?

✳✳✳

At any rate, back to Charles Taze Russell. Apparently he was a good speaker, because he was able to organize followers under different names, such as *Russellites, Millennial Dawnists and International Bible Students,* from all over the United States and Europe. One reason for his popularity could have been that he preached there was no hell. As part of his Bible research, he came up with the idea that the Hebrew term *sheol* did not mean *hell* as we have always believed, but *grave.* So everywhere he saw *hell* in the Bible, he just substituted *grave.* That's keen. Why don't we substitute for *punishment* in Scripture the term *ice cream*? I'll bet we'd become really popular.

This changing of Scripture to suit a purpose may have struck a key in Russell's spirit, because from the time this first concept of changing hell into grave was accepted, people not really wanting to consider their final resting place across the River Styx, he began his ministry of changing whatever he thought people didn't like. He traveled all over the country, preaching an average of six to eight hours a day.

His views were considered Adventist at the time. But with acceptance comes change. As his changes in Scripture were accepted, he made new changes, which were also accepted. He compiled a six-volume series called *Studies of the Scriptures* between 1886 and 1904.

He founded the Watch Tower Bible and Tract Society in 1884; then moved his headquarters from Pittsburgh to Brooklyn in 1909. William Taze Russell made a prediction that Christ was coming in 1914. When it didn't happen, Russell and his followers just claimed that the Christ[3] truly did come, only He was invisible. The people bought it; it did not seem to have an adverse effect on Russell's credibilty.

Russell was sort of an unusual person. Because he was rich, one can call him eccentric. But if he were not... Let the record speak for itself.

His wife sued him for divorce which was unheard of in those days. However, her charge was infidelity (adultery?) and cruelty. Did he subject her to his sermons before he gave them to his flock? We're not sure, but the court's declaration leaves one to wonder. It went like this:

*"...his course of conduct towards his wife evidences such **insistent egotism** and **extravagant self-praise** that it would be manifest to the jury that it would necessarily render the life of any sensitive Christian woman an intolerable burden."*

We've chosen to bold the key words in that statement to bring across our point regarding his behavior. Russell contested the divorce five times unsuccessfully.

He was also involved in some deals which we would

classify today as *"scams."*

● He was selling *"Miracle Wheat"* for $60 a bushel.

● He promoted a *"Cancer cure,"* consisting of a caustic paste of chloride of zinc, a wonderful *Millennial Bean*, and a *fantastic* cotton seed.[4]

To put the final chapter on the life of the founder of the Jehovah's Witnesses, Charles Taze Russell, and as possible tribute to his ultimate act of eccentricity, he died while riding a Santa Fe Railroad Pullman car in February, 1916. [Pullmans were private cars in which well-to-do people traveled all over the country in luxury. They were plush.] Russell had his own Pullman. He must have known the end was imminent. We don't know how for sure. He asked an associate to make him up a Roman toga, which he donned. He then raised up his legs and just passed on to his final reward.

✻✻✻

Joseph F. Rutherford - *Missouri Lawyer* 1869-1942

The truth to be known, Charles Taze Russell did not actually found the Jehovah's Witnesses. He is the father-in-faith of the group. But it was one of his followers, a very slick attorney named Joseph Franklin Rutherford who put it all together. In 1916, the year that Russell died, Rutherford was the legal adviser for the Watch Tower Bible and Tract Society. He had served in this capacity from the

Joseph F. Rutherford

inception of the soon to be Publishing Empire in 1906.

When Russell died, Rutherford became the president of the Watch Tower Society and leader of the Russellites. He slowly but systematically erased the name of Russell in the minds of all his followers and replaced it with his own. It was a touchy situation because Russell had thousands of followers who really loved him, or at least what they knew of him. As an example, Russell had come up with a concept that history could be predicted by measuring the rooms of the great Pyramids in Egypt. It's not said whether he or one of his followers actually measured the rooms in the great Pyramids, but it was a very real notion in Russell's mind and in many who followed him.

When Rutherford tried to debunk this theory, a lot of the old-timers reacted vehemently; but he was way ahead of them. He was building the enrollment of the *Russellites, International Bible and Tract People, Millennial Dawnists, Rutherfordites and then Watch Tower and Tract people.* The varied names of the different parts of the one organization caused some confusion, so in 1931, he came up with a new name to unite all aspects of the association. He called them the **Jehovah's Witnesses**. It's not readily understandable why they chose the name they did, but it became accepted by most members almost immediately. It's possible old Rutherford took a consensus of who thought what would be popular among all the people. At any rate, the name Jehovah's Witnesses stuck.

Rutherford lived an exotic life for a leader of a religious movement. He and seven other officers of the Watch Tower Society were indicted for espionage during World War I. They served nine months in an Atlanta Federal Penitentiary. Information is not readily available as to what the charges stemmed from. Obviously the charges stuck, because they were convicted and served time. After Rutherford was released from prison, he coined the name "Judge," which he called himself for the rest of his life. So you have "Pastor" for the man who was not a minister, and "Judge" for a man who was not part of the Judicial system. Not bad. After his prison stint, he also came up with a pet phrase, which he made popular, *"Millions Now Living Will Never Die."* The slogan soon appeared on all kinds of material, including road signs, advertising posters, handbills and the like.

He wrote twenty books and hundreds of pamphlets *attacking all Christianity*, but in particular the Catholic Church. Most of his writings were controversial and argumentative. He then turned much of it into recorded talks. He was really before his time. Today, audio cassettes are a major means of evangelization. But Rutherford was ahead of everybody. It was cumbersome for the Witnesses to run from door to door with portable phonographs to play his recordings; but they did! We're told they were short talks, but how short is short, especially if they're boring?

The *Watch Tower Society* in Brooklyn was called *Rutherford's Vatican*. But when he was not officiating there, he spent a lot of time in a mansion near San Diego, California. The property was in the name of Abel, Noah and Abraham. It was supposedly kept in readiness in the event any of the *owners* would ever decide to visit or come to lead the Witnesses in the great Battle of Armageddon. They never did. "Judge" Rutherford went to Jehovah in 1942. He had been extremely instrumental bringing about the growth of the Witnesses; at his death, there were approximately 100,000 members of the cult.

There was a dramatic increase in the number of Jehovah's Witnesses following the death of Rutherford and the end of the war. The two leaders following "Judge" Rutherford, Nathan Knorr, president until 1977, and Frederick Franz from 1977 until his death, were the movers and shakers which built the sleepy little group into a major religious figure. And it was all done door-to-door. Nathan Knorr was the one who instituted the outreach to foreign countries as well as setting up an organized training program. They had a bull by the horn and didn't know how to use it. Under Knorr's tutelage and Franz after him, they not only learned, they rode with it.

What Jehovah's Witnesses believe

The Jehovah's Witnesses book of beliefs is similar in many ways to the Adventists theology, but then they rear off and go their own way. Extra-Marital sex is taboo, as is the evolution or the big-bang theory of Creation. They also believe that Scripture is inspired by God, but they have taken the Bible and butchered it worse than Martin Luther did in his day. Their Bible has very little in common with our Bible. As an example:

Armageddon - Scripturally, Armageddon is the place spoken about in the Book of Revelations. The actual passage refers to the great war which will be fought there. *"They then assembled the kings in the place that is named Armageddon in Hebrew."*[5] Armageddon is prophesied to be the final battleground between good and evil at the end of the world. We want to quote the entire passage in which Armageddon plays a part.

"They then assembled the kings
in the place that is named Armageddon in Hebrew.
The seventh Angel poured out his bowl into the air.
A loud voice came out of the temple from the throne,
saying 'It is done.'
Then, there were lightning flashes,
rumblings, and peals of thunder, and a great earthquake.
It was such a violent earthquake
that there has never been one like it
since the human race began on earth.

The great city (Rome and the empire)
was split into three parts, and the gentile cities fell.
But God remembered great Babylon,
giving it the cup filled with the wine of His fury and
wrath."[6]

The **Jehovah's Witnesses** believe that everybody on earth will be killed except Jehovah's Witnesses. They say the Churches of Christendom will be the first to be destroyed. We don't see that in this Scripture passage. We're not sure where they got it. From the days of John, who wrote the book, it's been pretty much accepted that *"the great city"* and *"Babylon"* represents Rome and the Roman empire.

Birthdays are strictly forbidden.

Even sending birthday greeting cards are on the condemned list. Scriptural justification for this comes from:

Genesis 40:20-22 in which Pharaoh celebrated his birthday by hanging the chief baker.

Matthew 14:6, where Herod was having a birthday party at which the daughter of the queen danced an exotic dance, and manipulated Herod to kill John the Baptist as a gift to her.

Their thinking is that this is the only time that a birthday celebration is mentioned in Scripture. Both men were wicked; both men had someone killed on their birthday. Therefore, birthdays are evil. *Don't tell that to Mr. Hallmark!*

Blood Transfusions - are prohibited

You really have to use the imagination to come up with this no-no. The Society uses many Scripture passages to forbid blood transfusions. Some of those are:

Genesis 9:3-4 - *"Every creature that is alive shall be yours, yours to eat; I give them all to you as I did the green plants.*

Only flesh with its lifeblood still in it you shall

not eat."

Acts 15:28-29 - *"It is the decision of the Holy Spirit and of us not to place on you any burden beyond these necessities, namely, to abstain from meat sacrificed to idols, from blood, from meats of strangled animals, and from unlawful marriage. If you keep free of these, you will be doing what is right. Farewell."*

From this, the Jehovah Witnesses back in Brooklyn determined that a blood transfusion was akin to eating blood, **because** when we are fed intravenously, it *resembles* a blood transfusion.

Christianity - This gets a little confusing.

Jehovah's Witnesses teach that true Christianity departed from the earth shortly after the deaths of the Apostles, and didn't return until, guess when? 1914, when Jesus returned invisibly and found the only people practicing Christianity was Charles Taze Russell and his group. He then appointed them over Christianity. They maintain that He's been present since that time, but that His Second Coming will not occur until Armageddon comes. They also contend that those who witnessed the invisible return (contradiction in terms) in 1914, will not die until after He comes. Well, folks, assuming that these witnesses were adults in 1914, even teenagers, they will have to be turning 100 about now if they're still with us. Are we to believe that all these people are still alive and will stay alive until the Second Coming? *I don't think so!*

Now, we have to make a point here. With all this talk of being in charge of Christianity, Jesus having come in 1914, and coming back again, they don't believe that Jesus is the Messiah, or that He's the Son of God, or that He's Divine. So why all this talk of when He came and when He's coming back and what's going to happen?

There is something we have to understand as we go

through their beliefs and non-beliefs, through their understanding of Scripture. Words that we use do not mean the same thing to Jehovah's Witnesses as they do to Christians. Jesus, for instance, has a completely different meaning for us than He does for them.

Their belief in Jesus is as follows:

Christ was originally Michael the Archangel; He lived and died as a man and is now an exalted spirit.

Well, right off the bat, we disagree. Michael and the Angels are not men; they are pure spirit.[7] They continue:

> *"Prior to coming to earth, this only-begotten Son of God did not think himself to be co-equal with Jehovah God; he did not view himself as equal in power and glory' with Almighty God; he did not follow the course of the Devil and plot and scheme to make himself like or equal to the Most High God and to rob God or usurp God's place. On the contrary, he showed his subjection to God as his Superior by humbling himself under God's almighty hand, even to the most extreme degree, which means to a most disgraceful death on a torture stake."*[8]

Notice the word "torture stake" as opposed to the Cross. Their philosophy is that the Cross is a pagan symbol designed by the Catholic Church after Satan took over the world. They insist that Jesus was nailed to a straight upright pole. New Witness converts have to destroy any Crosses they have, not give them away, because the Witnesses hate the Cross.

***

St. René Goupil was the first North American Martyr. He was a doneé, a lay volunteer. He served in the Indian Missions in Canada and New York State. St. René made the Sign of the Cross on an Indian boy's head one day. The boy's grandfather, a chief in the tribe, saw St. René do this. He had two of his sons ambush St. René and tomahawk him. Then they threw his body into the river. This was in New York State, in a place called Auriesville, near Albany. Today, it's the Shrine of the North American Martyrs in the United States. The next day, the chief spoke to St. Isaac Jogues. He said, *"We hate when you make the Sign of the Cross. We kill you when you make the Sign of the Cross."* St. René Goupil died for the Cross. And these people call it a pagan symbol. We really are millions of miles apart.

✻✻✻

The Jehovah's Witnesses have truly taken Jesus of the Cross, as they, following the lead of their founder, call it a torture stake. Jesus was tortured and scourged before He took the Cross upon His Shoulders. It was upon the *Cross*, the One He carried laden with our sins, that He died for our salvation. They can call it anything they want, but it will not alter the fact He lived and He died for us, and it was on the Cross! This we Catholics believe! Following in the footsteps of their founder, they have made a practice of changing words in Scripture to accommodate their agenda.

Not to get on a patriotic bandwagon, but the Jehovah's Witnesses do not honor our country, *the United States of America,* in any way. They do not salute the American flag; they don't recite the Pledge of Allegiance, nor do they sing the National Anthem. Strangely enough, they do pay taxes. They do not serve in military service, vote or hold public office. They consider our government and all governments agents of the devil.

And because we are a free country, they are allowed to get away with this. Whenever they get into trouble with the government, the Jehovah's Witnesses get the ACLU to be their standard-bearers and come to their aid. Then they turn around and call the ACLU the devil's agent. There's some sort of *comeuppance* there, I think.

In Jehovah's Witness land, Satan was cast out of

heaven and now rules the world; he is gathering his forces for the big battle of Armageddon; his greatest allies comprise members of the religious of the world, especially Christian religions, Catholic and Protestant; they also include members of the commercial world and politicians. The faithful Witnesses will not take part in the big battle of Armageddon. They will sit on a mountainside and watch while Jesus and the angels overcome Satan and his cohorts.

The righteous survivors will marry and go forth and multiply during the remaining years of the 1000 year period. *[I thought they were all up on a mountain, and that this was a spectator sport. How come there are survivors, survivors of what?]* The dead will stay dead until the resurrection. The evil ones will be exterminated. *[That includes all but those who are* Jehovah's Witnesses.]

At the end of the 1000 year period, they anticipate billions of people will have been reproduced, most or all Jehovah's Witnesses. Satan will now be allowed to roam the earth again for one last sweep. Anyone who is lured into his trap will be destroyed with Satan and his ilk. The rest will live on earth forever. We're told it is to be a Garden of Eden type atmosphere. So we're assuming the Witnesses will live happily ever after, while the rest of us have died.

Now here's where we get into a sticky, or a little confusing part of the equation. *Heaven!* The billions who have reproduced over the 1000 year period are not going to Heaven. There's only room for 144,000 and most of them are already waiting in line. There is a belief that as of 1985, there were only about 9,000 who were guaranteed to be in that number, when the saints go marching in.

We want you to look at some figures that were compiled, based on their annual communion service, which takes place all over the world.

In 1920, they began taking a role of how many

volunteers there were working for the Society. There's an interesting pattern which we would like to point out to you. According to the figures we've been given:

	Volunteers	attend annual communion	partake
1920	8,042		
1938	59,047	69,345	36,732.
1948	260,756	376,393	25,395.
1958	798,326	1,171,789	15,037.
1974	2,179,256	4,925,643	10,550.
1985	3,024,131	7,792,109	9,051.

Notice how according to these figures,[9] the enrollment went up dramatically over the years. From 1920 to 1985, the volunteer count went from 8,042 to 3,024,131. Those who went to their annual communion went from 69,345 in 1938 to 7,792,109 in 1985. But those who partook of the communion declined from 36,732 in 1938 to 9,051 in 1985. The decline would not be so dramatic if the increase in attendance had not been so great. In 1938, out of 69,345 who attended, 36,732 partook of the communion. That's 53%, over half. In 1985, out of 7,792,109 who attended, only 9,051 partook of the communion. That's like 1/12 of a per cent.

We understand why fewer than the total membership partake of communion. Only those who are considered worthy are allowed to receive. But look at the enormous increase in membership and the drastic decrease in those who are considered worthy to partake communion. Either that little number was all that was left in 1985 of the original 36,732 from 1938, or their new people are not worthy of receiving. Are these also the ones who will not go to Heaven? It gets a little confusing.

Their Kingdom Halls have become almost convention center size. They meet twice a week in these halls for their services. But they're not really services as much as meetings where they go over activities, progress reports, and study the Watch Tower propaganda. There is a certain amount of prayer, but it's not the major activity of the evening.

Resurrection - Jehovah Witnesses do not believe in the Resurrection.
They say that when Jesus died, He became a non-person; He ceased to exist. On the third day, He resurrected as an angel. But His Body never came back. However, they do maintain that the invisible Jesus came in 1914, and brought some dead people *to a spirit life* at that time, not Heaven, but a spirit life. The rest will be raised bodily after the *"thousand-year reign."*

[These Witnesses use the Bible to turn the innocent away from their churches, but completely ignore it when it is contrary to their theology. If for example, as they say, Jesus' Body did not rise, how do they account for Holy Scripture which says, Jesus ate with the disciples (in the Upper room) on the day he rose from the dead, and then by the Sea of Galilee; Thomas was told to place his hands in Jesus' *Side*. He had to have had a Body for all this to have come to pass.]

The Trinity - To the Jehovah's, the Trinity is ridiculous.
In one of their books, *Let God Be True*,[10] they refer to the Trinity in this way:
*"When the clergy are asked by their followers as to how such a combination of three in one can possibly exist, they are obliged to answer, `That is a mystery.' Some will try to illustrate it by using triangles, trefoils, or images with three heads on one neck. Nevertheless, sincere persons who want to know the true God and serve him find it a bit difficult to love and worship a complicated, **freakish-looking, three-headed God**. The clergy who inject such ideas will contradict themselves in the very next breath by stating that God made man*

in his own image; for certainly no one has ever seen a ***three-headed human creature.***"[11]

To all ***Christians***, especially in the Catholic Church, The Holy Trinity is extremely important. The Catechism of the Catholic Church, one of the most powerful books on our Faith, describes the Trinity as the:

"central mystery of Christian faith and life. It is the mystery of God in Himself. It is therefore, the source of all the other mysteries of Faith, the light that enlightens them. It is the most fundamental and essential teaching in the `hierarchy of the Truths of Faith.'[12,]"[13]

Everything we do begins with the Trinity: God the Father, God the Son and God the Holy Spirit.[14]

Holy Spirit - For Witnesses the Holy Spirit does not exist.

They relegate the Holy Spirit to an *"active force"* that Jehovah God uses to do His bidding.

Whereas the **Catholic Church** has this to say about the Holy Spirit, and it all comes from Scripture:

"And in the last days it shall be, God declares, that I will pour out My Spirit upon all flesh, and your sons and your daughters shall prophesy, and your young men shall see visions, and your old men shall dream dreams;[15]

And I will show wonders in the Heavens above and signs on the earth beneath,..."[16]

In the *Old Testament* it was believed that the Holy Spirit rested on the hoped-for Messiah. When Jesus was baptized by John in the Jordan River and the Holy Spirit descended upon Him, this was the sign that He was the Messiah, the Son of God.[17]

Our Lord *Jesus* prophesied the outpouring of the Holy Spirit on the Apostles and Disciples, on many occasions. As the Word is alive for all time, like God without limitations of time and space, so these words are for us, too.

"...do not worry about how to defend yourselves or what you are to say, because when the time comes, the Holy Spirit will teach you what you must say."[18]

"I tell you most solemnly, unless a man is born through water and the Spirit, he cannot enter the kingdom of God; what is born of the flesh is flesh; what is born of the Spirit is spirit. Do not be surprised when I say; You must be born from above. The wind blows wherever it pleases; you hear its sound, but you cannot tell where it comes from or where it is going. That is how it is with all who are born of the Spirit."[19]

"Still, I must tell you the truth; it is for your own good that I am going, because unless I go, the Advocate will not come to you; but if I do go, I will send Him to you."[20]

"But when the Spirit of truth comes He will lead you to the complete truth, since He will not be speaking as from Himself, but will say only what He has learned; and He will tell you of the things to come. He will glorify Me, since all He tells you will be taken from what is Mine."[21]

"...but you will receive power when the Holy Spirit comes on you, and then you will be My witnesses not only in Jerusalem but throughout Judea and Samaria, and indeed to the ends of the earth."[22]

As you can see, Jehovah Witnesses do not believe according to the Bible, as they profess.[23]

Holidays - To the Witnesses, this is like a dirty word.

It saddens us so, when one of their children cannot accept gifts for their birthdays or at Christmas Time. [Our grandchildren gave us a beautiful hanging which says the greatest gift God the Father gave us was His son wrapped in swaddling clothes.] Needless to say, they do not celebrate Christmas, calling it a pagan holiday. Reminds us of the serpent in the Garden of Eden when he called God a liar. And so, poor souls, they are deprived of the Gift of God's Son and most of God's gifts (Graces) because of a philosophy that began with one man's dangerous theology, and has been perpetuated by those who have followed.

Well when you think about this cult's focus, rejecting holidays makes sense. They want their people working all day long, every day, 365 days a year. In their Brooklyn sweat shop, they have anywhere from 1,500 to 2,000 Witnesses living in an apartment owned by the Society. They work in the print factory. They do everything: press work, setting type, binding books, mail, anything it takes to run the national headquarters. For this they are given room and board, and $20 per month which they should not spend frivolously.

Therefore in order to justify this *workaholic philosophy*, they need to claim that holidays are tools of the devil, used to worship pagan rituals. Even those that do not fall into the category of pagan rituals are forbidden because *"carnal people celebrate them."* Nice people! The *carnal people* they are referring to are all Christians!

They replace the Name of God with Jehovah.

The Witnesses do not refer to God as God, but in most instances have replaced His Name with Jehovah. Other areas where our beliefs differ strongly are:

Sacraments - Jehovah's Witnesses deny the Sacraments.

Whereas the *Catholic Church* teaches:

Sacraments are *"Powers that come forth"* from the Body of Christ, which is ever-living and life-giving. They are actions of the Holy Spirit at work in His Body, the Church. They are *"the masterworks of God"* in the new and everlasting covenant.[24]

The Catechism of the Catholic Church, in quoting from the Council of Trent, teaches that all Sacraments were instituted by Jesus Christ our Lord. The actual passage from the Council of Trent is as follows:

> *"If anyone shall say that the Sacraments of the New Law were not all instituted by Jesus Christ our Lord, or that there are more or less than seven, namely Baptism; Confirmation, Eucharist, Penance, Extreme Unction;*[25] *Holy Orders, and Matrimony, or even that anyone of these seven is not truly and strictly speaking a Sacrament, let him be anathema."*[26]

"'Seated at the right hand of the Father' and pouring out the Holy Spirit on His Body, which is the Church, Christ now acts through the Sacraments He instituted to communicate His grace. The Sacraments are perceptible signs (words and actions) accessible to our human nature. By the action of Christ and the power of the Holy Spirit they make present efficaciously[27] the grace that they signify."[28,29]

Baptism - Jehovah's Witnesses don't consider Baptism a Sacrament, although they perform a baptism of sorts at large meetings. They christen on beaches and river banks. But to them, there is no Sacramental importance attached to these things.

In the **Catholic Church**, Baptism is the first Sacrament we receive, opening wide the window of our souls to the Grace of God, welcoming the Holy Spirit to dwell within us. It is the doorway through which the other Sacraments enter. It is the Sacrament of *regeneration* and *renewal* in the Holy Spirit; because it brings about the birth of water and the Spirit which Jesus speaks of to Nicodemus, when He tells him that without this *rebirth* no one can enter into the Kingdom of God.[30]

Eucharist - Jehovah Witnesses don't believe in the Eucharist
They don't acknowledge the Real Presence of Jesus in the Eucharist. But they do have an annual communion

service, in which the *elect* partake of bread and wine. This date has to coincide with the 14th day of Nisan, which is their equivalent of our Good Friday. But this is not the Eucharist as we know It or believe.

The Eucharist, to the **Catholic Church**, is the most important of the Sacraments. In the Catechism of the Catholic Church, we read that which we have believed from the very beginning, that it is through the presence of Jesus in our midst, the Eucharist, that we have that union between Heaven and earth and through that union the Church has survived 2000 years of persecution, in one form or the other. It is through that union that hell has not prevailed against Christ's Church.

"The unity of the Mystical Body: the Eucharist makes the Church. Those who receive the Eucharist are united more closely to Christ. Through it Christ unites them to all the faithful in one body - the Church. Communion renews, strengthens, and deepens this incorporation into the Church, already achieved through Baptism. In Baptism we have been called to form but one body. The Eucharist fulfills this call: 'The cup of blessing we bless, is it not a participation in the Blood of Christ? The Bread which we break, is it not a participation in the Body of Christ? Because there is one Bread, we who are many are one body, for we all partake of the one Bread.' [31],"[32]

St. Paul, in this letter to the Corinthians plainly states that the cup is *Blood* and the Bread is the *Body* of Christ. He goes on to say that it is through the partaking of that one Loaf, the sharing of the Body and Blood of Christ, the Eucharist, that we are one body (unity).

"At the Last Supper, on the night He was betrayed, our Savior instituted the Eucharistic sacrifice of His Body and Blood. This He did in order to perpetuate

the Sacrifice of the Cross throughout the ages until He should come again, and so entrust to His beloved Spouse, the Church, a memorial of His death and resurrection: a Sacrament of Love, a sign of unity, a bond of charity, a Paschal banquet; in which Christ is consumed, the mind is filled with grace, and a pledge of future glory is given to us."[33]

What was required for our salvation was the Sacrifice of the Perfect Lamb, the Son of God - Our Lord Jesus, the Sacrifice that took place and was culminated on the Cross. The Eucharist comes to us through the ongoing Sacrifice of the Cross, the Sacrifice of the Mass where the victim-priest "*in persona Christi*," offers sacrifice to the Father, doing it in remembrance of Him, as Jesus commanded the night of the Last Supper. And it is through the Eucharist that man is saved and has eternal life.[34]

Marriage - Witnesses do not consider Marriage a sacrament

As they do not believe in Sacraments, marriage between two people is merely a contract entered into, according to the civil laws of the country in which they live. This is interesting, that they accept the laws in this instance! But we find it strange that they don't embrace Marriage as being more important than they do.

Is it not true that marriage[35] gives us family; family gives us membership; membership gives us strength? Is this not why there has been such an attack by Satan and his cohorts on *Marriage* and family, to destroy the Church by destroying the family. The Catholic Church teaches: Marriage has always played an important part in Salvation History. The Catechism of the Catholic Church tells us:

"Sacred Scripture begins with the creation of man and woman in the image and likeness of God and concludes with a vision of `the Wedding Feast of the Lamb.'"

"*So the Lord God cast a deep sleep on the man, and while he was asleep, He took out one of his ribs and closed up its place with flesh. The Lord God then built up into a woman the rib that He had taken from the man. When He brought her to the man, the man said:*
'*This one, at last, is bone of my bones*
and flesh of my flesh;
This one shall be called woman
for out of 'her man' this one has been taken.'
That is why a man leaves his father and mother and clings to his wife, and the two of them become one flesh."[36]

Then again at the end of Scripture in the Book of Revelation:

"*Let us rejoice and be glad and give Him glory.*
For the wedding day of the Lamb has come,
His bride has made herself ready."[37]
and then again:

"*Then the Angel said to me: 'Write this: Blessed are those who have been called to the wedding feast of the Lamb.'*

"*And he said to me, 'These words are true; they come from God.'*"[38]

It goes on to say that "*Scripture speaks throughout of Marriage and its 'mystery,'*"[39] its institution and the meaning God has given it, its origin and its end, its various realizations throughout the history of salvation, the difficulties arising from sin and its renewal '*in the Lord*' in the New Covenant of Christ and the Church."[40]

In the introduction to the Sacraments, we spoke of how the Sacraments of *Holy Orders* and *Matrimony* have been grouped together as specially Consecrated Sacraments. Holy Orders was created by Jesus Christ Himself at the Last Supper. Matrimony was created by God the Father in the Garden of Eden at the very beginning of Salvation History.

Marriage has played an important part down through the millenniums with regard to Salvation and Redemption.

From a very logical viewpoint, the Sacrament of Marriage, the couple joined to each other with God and the Church Community as witness, are what creates family. The Church depends on family for its very existence. The family of God builds the Church with its members, supports the Church with its time and talents, builds the buildings with its donations and ultimately feeds the ministries of the Church with its children, especially the priesthood. The Church depends on the family for its very survival.[41]

Salvation - Witnesses believe we are not saved by God.
They believe that we are not saved by the Grace of God, but by our own merits - the work that we do for our salvation. However, in no event are more than the 144,000 elect saved. The rest of the Witnesses will live in a Garden-of-Eden type of existence after the 1000 year reign.

Soul - Jehovah's Witnesses do not believe the Soul exists.
They vacillate. Some of their books say there is a soul, while the party line is that it does not exist; in any event, it's not immortal. Immortality is only given to those who have merited it by faithfully following the Jehovah's Witnesses' rules. Whether they are only the 144,000, or they include those billions who have given their all to the movement, but will only live in the near-perfect Garden of Eden, is not clear; it fluctuates based on what they're selling.

Church - Witnesses contend Jesus did not found a church.
They give no value to the early Christian Church. They have no use for a church; they believe it is worthless and an impediment to salvation.

Ethics and Morals - are based on needs of the movement
They are based subjectively, by the Jehovah's Witnesses, adjusted to the times and focus of the organization

at any given time. The Witnesses do not out and out condemn smoking, drinking and movies, except if the money could have been spent for the Witnesses, and the time given to do something for the movement.

Education is not a big thing with the Jehovah's Witnesses, other than learning everything that the Society puts out. College is not recommended; they don't look for college students. Their outreach is to the educationally challenged, and to minority groups. They do very well with Hispanics: Puerto Ricans, Cubans and Mexicans. Most of their people live outside the United States in places like Puerto Rico, Mexico, Brazil, the Philippines, and more recently in African countries. Wherever there are the minority groups, the Jehovah's Witnesses are there, with their snares.

Everyone works!

There are no handouts. Anyone who joins the Witnesses is a very active member, or they're not Jehovah's Witnesses. Once they get converts, they keep them working. A convert takes bible, speech and salesmanship courses, is indoctrinated into missionary procedures early on. Within a short period of time, they're out there, ringing doorbells with an experienced Witness along. An average Witness has to attend five hourly meetings a week and devotes at least ten hours a month witnessing door-to-door. These are called *Kingdom Publishers*. Then there are those who are called *Pioneers*. They have to donate a *hundred hours* per month to the Society. *That's averaging twenty-five hours per week!* And they don't get paid anything!

We have been able to determine certain tracts they use from our years of exposure to them. In recent years, we would see a young woman, in her mid-forties, an older woman, possibly a Hispanic, and a child as part of the team. When we tell them we're Catholic, they'll either say they *were* Catholic or one of their relatives *was* Catholic. But that's not unusual. All the proselytizers do the same, the Seventh Day Adventist, even the Mormons.

The last time we were accosted by them at our home, they had the young woman, the older woman and a little girl. The only one who had blood flowing through her veins was the older, Hispanic woman. The other two were robots. First, when we said we were Catholic, the young woman hit Penny with *"My husband used to be Catholic."* Penny said, *"Tell your husband he's condemned because he knows Whom he denied when he left the Catholic Church to become a Witness. He has denied Jesus, his God!"* The young woman flatly admitted, *"We don't believe that Jesus is God."* Whereupon Penny demanded, *"Do you tell Catholics that you don't believe in Jesus when you're proselytizing?"* The woman answered, *"Most Catholics don't know as much as you do about their Faith."* Penny responded, *"Well, you're condemned, too, if, before you start reeling Catholics into your cult, you don't tell them to go and learn about their own Faith, so they know what they're giving up when they join you."*

Penny started to share the beauty of our Church. The child and the young woman were like stone. But at one point, when Penny was sharing about our love for Jesus, we could see tears welling up in the eyes of the older woman. Was it something she remembered, something she had buried deep in her heart, not daring to open the chest which contained the Truth she had learned as a child?

I think they must have a network, which tells them who to go to, and who not to go to. We haven't seen any Jehovah's Witnesses from that time to this.

✳✳✳

They are a committed group of people, these Jehovah's Witnesses. The writings of the founders, *"Pastor"* Russell and *"Judge"* Rutherford are not to be found. As a matter of fact, all their Watchtower articles and books are anonymous. They are totally integrated into the work they do. Nothing else is important; everything else is a distraction. For Catholics, whom they hate by the way, they are deadly; and don't for a minute think they are not formidable adversaries. One person, William J. Whalen, who reported on the Jehovah's Witnesses[42] had this to say in warning:

"...the Scriptural gymnastics of a trained Witness is a sure sign of godliness. What matter if this 'minister' never finished high school, knows no Biblical languages, chooses to quote out of context? As a matter of fact anyone who itches to engage an experienced Witness in a Biblical duel had better make sure he has spent as much time memorizing proof passages...as his opponent."

Pride is Satan's greatest enemy. Don't think you're up to competing with these people on a one-to-one basis. Remember, they've been in training. They have only one goal, to take your soul away from you and make you a Jehovah's Witness carbon copy . Don't let it happen. Find out how you can go out with members of your own church, through the Legion of Mary or some other outreach group, to combat these people with the true Word of God. Jesus needs you; your Church needs you!

Footnotes

[1]Rev 22:18-19
[2]American Family Foundation, Boston, MA
[3]not to be confused with the Jesus in whom we believe - theirs is a completely different concept of Jesus
[4]Separated Brethren - William J. Whalen - Our Sunday Visitor
[5]Rev 16:16
[6]Rev 16:16-19

[7]St. Thomas Aquinas, Summa Theologiae
[8]Let God Be True, 2nd Edition - Watch Tower Society, Pg 34
[9]Jehovah's Witnesses - David A. Reed - Baker Book House
[10]Watch Tower Bible & Tract Society 1946 - Pg. 34
[11]certain words bolded by author to emphasize a point
[12]General Catholic Directory #43
[13]Catechism of the Catholic Church #234
[14]Read the Chapter on the Trinity in *Trilogy Book I - Treasures of the Church*
[15]Acts 2:17
[16]Acts 2:19
[17]Jn 1:33-34
[18]Lk 12:12
[19]Jn 3:5-8
[20]Jn 16:7
[21]Jn 16-13-14
[22]Acts 1:8
[23]Chapter on the Holy Spirit in *Trilogy Book I - Treasures of the Church*
[24]Catechism of the Catholic Church #1116
[25]Now called the Anointing of the Sick
[26]Council of Trent (1547): DS 1601
[27]producing the desired effect
[28]Catechism of the Catholic Church #1084
[29]Chapter on Sacraments *Trilogy Book I - Treasures of the Church*
[30]*cf* Jn 3:5 - in Chapter on Baptism *Trilogy Book I - Treasures of the Church*
[31]1Cor 10:16,17
[32]Catechism of the Catholic Church #1396
[33]Catechism of the Catholic Church #1323
[34]Chapter on Eucharist *Trilogy Book I - Treasures of the Church*
[35] A Sacrament - the Sacrament of Matrimony, according to the Catholic Church
[36]Gen 2:21-24
[37]Rev 19:7
[38]Rev 19:9
[39]Eph 5:32
[40]Catechism of the Catholic Church #1602
[41]Chapter on Marriage *Trilogy Book I - Treasures of the Church*
[42]Separated Brethren - Our Sunday Visitor

Seventh Day Adventists

Although some accept *Seventh Day Adventists* as Christians, we chose not to place them with *Main-Line Protestant denominations* who are separated from us by the *Tragedy of the Reformation*,[1] as they did not stem from that terrible tragedy but instead radicalized all Lutheran and Calvinist concepts, drawing them even a farther distance from the Church Jesus left to His children. We have placed them and the others following, under the category of Sects because they were begun by men through an alleged vision, linking its beginning and reason for existence to *Mysticism*. There is also another very important difference: *Main-Line Protestant denominations*, unlike sects such as the Adventists, do not proselytize (to brainwash, indoctrinate, prejudice, sway) Catholics, or *other Protestant denominations*, with the express purpose of pressuring them to leave their Church. Therefore, we have made the decision to link those denominations not from the Reformation under the category of either *Sects or Cults*.

Seventh Day Adventists

Our first and only experience with this sect was when our Ministry was solely a Pilgrimage Ministry. We received a phone call from someone inquiring if we could give him some figures on cost to bring a group to the Holy Land. In later conversations, he revealed he represented the Seventh Day Adventists. Now, I must admit I wondered how we who only bring out Catholic Pilgrimages could be of service; but then I thought, well we are all Christians, at that time not knowing denominations from sects and sects from cults. Luz Elena did a lot of research on air fares and land prices from our resources in the Holy Land. She set up a Pilgrimage program visiting all the Shrines we went to when we brought out our Pilgrimages to the Holy Land.

After receiving all her figures and giving them to the man, he told her he was quite pleased with all she had done and desired a meeting. He suggested we come to his office in the neighboring town. When we approached the address he had given us, it was a big complex surrounded by walls and a gated entrance. We could not believe our eyes! Spread out before us were rolling hills of acres and acres of new, modern buildings everywhere we looked. There were television studios, and printing plants, buildings devoted to an outreach through the printed word in books and magazines. A large sign greeted us: *Seventh Day Adventists.* A receptionist ushered us into a huge, plush office. A very clean-cut, well dressed man rose from behind a huge mahogany desk and greeted us warmly. He reiterated what he had said on the phone, commending the outstanding job we had done. Then he said: *"Your price is better than the other bid we received; your itinerary is far superior and I am ready to sign a contract guaranteeing you 4000 pilgrims a year."*

Bob's first reaction was, *"We died and went to Heaven."* Then Penny thought to herself: *"My Mama used to say: 'Beware Greeks bearing gifts.' Well, this guy was not Greek, but was I naive or should I have wondered if this was not the devil himself offering us something that was too good to be true? To make matters worse, we really needed that account."*

He had fed us the bait; now he would reel us in. He continued: *"The only problem is that you are Catholic and the owners of the other company bidding, are members of our church. Now, I used to be Catholic, and my family is still Catholic; but I saw the truth. How would you like to join us. You would get all our travel and we do a great deal of travelling."* He was smooth, but what he didn't know was that we had given up the world and all its entrapments; we were not about to serve Satan by *betraying* our Church and all that we believe in. We politely thanked him for his offer and said that we were born Catholic and we would die Catholic.

Who are the Seventh Day Adventists?

Seventh Day Adventists stemmed from the original group, called the Adventists. They were Christians who believed that the Second Coming of Christ was imminent, like very soon. They also believed in the Sabbath being Saturday, rather than Sunday. They made a very big thing about this, condemning the Catholic Church for having changed it from Saturday to Sunday, and also condemning any Protestant groups who worshiped the Sabbath as being on Sunday.

They preach a final battle between the forces of good and evil, identified as the Biblical Battle of Armageddon. Jesus will be victorious in that battle, at which time, He will establish a 1,000 year kingdom in the Biblical city of Jerusalem. The earth will be uninhabited for that thousand years, and at the end, Jesus will bring the New Jerusalem to earth and we will all live in peace and love for eternity. Satan and all the wicked will be destroyed.

Basically there are *four persons* responsible for the founding of this sect which has become a formidable threat to Catholics as well as Protestants, the most vulnerable being Hispanics and widows or single mothers, in need of financial and/or emotional assistance. Often sects like this come through when to our shame we Catholics fail our brothers and sisters in need. Now, I would commend their horizontal generosity, but the price! They hit people when they are most vulnerable, giving them all they need and then it doesn't take too much, especially if the person does not know his own Faith, to get them to leave their Church and go with these *nice* people. There is a price tag to their generosity. It may not be money but it could be your soul.

William Miller - a peasant turned prophet

William Miller was born in Pittsfield, Massachusetts in 1782. His family moved to Low Hampton, New York while he was still quite young. They were farmers. Now they were God-fearing Christians who brought up their son to go to church and obey the Bible; but as soon as this highly spirited young man was old enough, he stopped believing in the Bible, became a complete agnostic, and enlisted in the Army. This is not too unusual; often when we are young we are easily tossed here and there by the wind, until we settle down.

His stint in the services over, William returned home and joined the *Baptist Church*. His skepticism gone, he began digging into the Bible. Now when we read Holy Scripture without the proper guidance of a priest or a Catholic Concordance, we are leaving ourselves open to error. If what Luther had said was right, that everyone is capable of interpreting the Word of God for himself, why do we have so many different denominations all claiming they are following the Word, all preaching something else? What happened with William Miller is so typical of the indiscriminate student of the Bible. Miller came up with what he interpreted as the Lord's message to him. Based on this, he affected many lives. Now, there is no question that while at least in the beginning, he had good intentions, he really didn't know what he was talking about.

After two years of pouring through the Bible, not the Catholic Bible, but the King James version which is missing seven books, he said the Lord told him, through His Word, that within 25 years, something was going to come about that would end the world's suffering. This was his interpretation of passages from Daniel in the Old Testament and Revelation in the New Testament. These are two of the most difficult books of the Bible to interpret. Scripture scholars admit they are too symbolic for the common man to venture to understand.

What Miller really wanted to say was that the world was coming to an end and everyone should prepare for *Jesus' Second Coming*. But although he was convinced this was what was revealed to him and that it was from the Lord, he was afraid to tell anyone else, in so many words. To his great amazement, when he did divulge what the Lord had disclosed to him, it was not only accepted, it drew huge crowds of people. They jammed into large assembly halls, filling them beyond capacity. What drew them? His message: *Twenty five more years and the world will come to an end!* [Now do not think harshly of these people or judge them any more fools than those today who run after every alleged mystic who claims the end of the world is going to happen on this day, and that day passing, on another day.]

Now, he said that with the end of the world, prosperity would come; no more sickness, no more poverty, no more materialism; everyone would have plenty and everyone would share all that he had with his brother. The Lord was coming and with Him, the Kingdom of God on earth! This, according to his calculations was going to take place between March 21st, 1843 and March 21st, 1844. Imagine the excitement! People sold their homes, gave away all their earthly possessions, donned white robes and began looking toward the heavens. Their Lord was coming and they wanted to be ready!

✳ ✳ ✳

I couldn't help thinking about the poor deluded souls who at the end of the *20th century* in San Diego, California, were donning travelling clothes and running shoes as *their prophet* had foretold they would be beamed up to Heaven,[2] as I was writing about the people who had believed the first prophet of the Adventists, and upon whose prophecy the authority of the Adventists stands. They too gave up all they possessed, donned white robes and looked up toward the heavens for Jesus to come, at any moment. We in no way want to cast aspersions on anyone's belief. It's just that if we do not speak up and let you know *what they believe*, and souls are lost, all because we wanted to be liked, we share in the offense. We are our brother's keeper!

✵ ✵ ✵

But first March 21st, 1843 came and no Lord. The days passed into weeks, and the weeks into months, and the very last day - March 21st, 1844 came and no Lord. Imagine the disappointment which soon turned into anger. In a desperate attempt to buy time, the date was recalculated to be October 22, 1844. But when Jesus did not come on that day, William Miller was finished as a prophet.

History tells us that Miller spoke with no intention of leading his followers astray; after the time came and passed, he confessed his error and expressed deep sorrow that he had disappointed them; but he *stressed* they must be prepared, for the Lord was coming and the time was fast approaching. Was he insincere? I think not; if anything, he was not knowledgeable of the Word of God, that's obvious. But what came to pass happens whenever preachers, or anyone else, base their interpretations of the Bible on what (they believe) the Spirit is saying to them, rather than relying on what the Church, who chose these Scriptures in the first place, teaches.

Well sincere or not, this ended William Miller's revered place in the sect as prophet and preacher.

But that was not the end of the story. New prophets quickly rose from the ashes, and defended *prophecies* which had not come to pass but were the essence of their entire belief, as they contended that the end of the world *was forthcoming*, and that William Miller *had received* the prophecy; but the problem was that he had not properly interpreted it; that's why the Lord had raised *them* up, to bring the members the time and place, when it was revealed to them, the new prophets. But the strange thing was that the *new* prophets who followed were able to keep the old membership and gain new ones, promoting the very same prophecies that disappointed them in the first place and got Miller thrown out. However, they did not specify a date, as had Miller.

Enter **Hiram Edson**, prophet #2, with a new prophecy: *"I saw the Lord entering the holiest place."* Now Hiram was one of the new prophets who was certain the Lord's coming was just around the corner. When it didn't happen, he called together some of the membership and they prayed all night. Suddenly he reported he had seen the sky open and the *High Priest*, instead of coming out of His *heavenly shrine* into a shrine on *earth*, entered a second room of His celestial shrine. He said that Miller's prophecy had been right, but in misinterpreting it, what he had not known was that what the Lord had revealed to him was that He was not coming to purify an earthly shrine, but a shrine in Heaven. [There is such a problem with that, as Heaven is perfect. How can you, why would you, purify that which is perfect?]

Nevertheless, people always longing for God or any word from Him, the sect grew in New York[3] because of this explanation, and Edson's fame along with it.

Enter a new prophet! **Joseph Bates** had been touched during his long assignment on the seas and had converted to Christianity. When he retired from being a seaman, Bates took this movement to Washington and New Hampshire. Convinced this was the way for him, he began to zealously and tirelessly promote the Adventist church. One of his main focuses was to advocate the sacredness of the Lord's day. He is considered the main one responsible for the Adventists keeping holy the Sabbath. Now, in accord with how *he* interpreted the Lord's Word, Bates insisted that the Bible pointed to the Lord's day being Saturday, not Sunday (as all Christians believe and keep holy).

In 1846, he wrote a book expounding his theory keeping holy Saturday as the Sabbath. That being successfully accepted, he went on to publish a second version, including not only his theory on the sabbath, but adding a vicious attack on the Catholic Church and the Papacy, manipulating Scripture to suit his own purposes. He accused the Pope of being the *beast* in Revelations 14:6-20. Now the Bible reads: *"All those who worship the beast...."* We Catholics do not worship the Pope or anyone on earth or in Heaven except God. Therefore, we cannot fit the bill of those whom St. John is speaking. And since we do not, neither does the Pope. Bates used the passage where St. John wrote *"Babylon has fallen. The great Babylon has fallen."*[4] to attack the Church in Rome, as Luther, Calvin and other heretics before him, calling the Church Babylon. Whereas, it has always been the accepted belief, from the days of the Early Church (when St. John wrote Revelation), that St. John was referring to *Nero's Rome* as Babylon. And Nero's Rome has indeed fallen, and Bate's Babylon - our Church still stands and always will stand, because Jesus Who is the Word made that promise that hell would not prevail against her. And Bates and all those who have followed, although they have tried and tried, will not bring about her fall.

Again, success and acceptance, the foolish always looking for someone and something to tickle their ears, another blasphemous book is published, and once again accepted. Only this one, again Bates stuck in Revelation, interprets John as proclaiming that only the elect, that number being 144,000 will be the sealed ones.[5]

But in St. John's Revelation,[6] *144* refers to the twelve tribes of Israel multiplied by twelve making 144, multiplied by 1000 making 144,000 symbolizing the *New Israel* - the Roman Catholic Church, which embraces people from every nation, race and tongue. And then in St. Paul's letter to the Galatians,[7] *"Peace and mercy to all who follow this rule and to the Israel of God,"* St. Paul is referring to the Catholic Church as the Israel of God.

In Revelation,[8] John presents a gentle, loving comforting picture of the Lamb for His people. In Jerusalem, it has always been the tradition that the *true remnant* of Jesus' followers, the Israel of faith (another name for the Catholic Church), will be gathered on Mount Zion, when Our Lord Jesus Christ comes again. In Rev. 7:4-9, when John speaks of those who are marked with the seal, he is speaking of those having God the Father's name on their foreheads, in contrast to the pagans who will be recognized by the name or number of the beast on their foreheads. [When John speaks of those who bear the Father's Name on their foreheads, he is referring to Catholics who are anointed on their foreheads during three of the *Sacraments*: *Baptism*, *Confirmation* and *Extreme Unction*.]

St. James writes: *"James, a slave of God and of the Lord Jesus Christ, to the twelve tribes in the Dispersion,[9] greetings."*[10] When James calls himself a slave of God and of the Lord Jesus Christ, he is declaring himself an authority commissioned to instruct Christ's Church (the only one being the Church He founded - The Roman Catholic Church).

Did Joseph Bates know this? Worse, did the poor deluded who followed him know? Are we silent today when so many of our beloved brothers and sisters, not knowing the Truth fall prey to sects and cults?

Ellen White has been called *The Mother of Adventism* as she is looked upon as the real founder of the Adventists. Ellen was born into the Harmon family, in Maine, in 1827. At nine years old, when she was coming home from school, she was struck in the face by a stone and was unconscious for three weeks. Her nervous system was severely damaged by this occurrence, and she suffered from that time on. She, along with her family, belonged to the Methodist Church, when at the age of thirteen, she heard William Miller preach in Portland, Maine. This started her on her road toward mysticism and the Adventists. Not long after, she began having visions, *many* visions!

Again the people were looking for word from the Lord, and not knowing where to find it, Ellen became an overnight success. People flocked to hear her speak, filling huge tents and auditoriums. They sat spell-bound, motionless, as they listened to her describe her phenomenal encounters with the *beyond*. She lifted their spirits, as she reassured them the revelations, foretold by the other prophets (of the Adventists) before her, were reliable and would come to pass, soon. They had begun to lose faith in the prophecies and the prophets, but here was Ellen having visions supporting what had been told. She was able to transport them into what *"would be,"* taking their minds off the *"what was,"* when she spoke of the Second Coming of the Lord.

The focus of her mission was to validate Miller's prophecy. She preached that the date that he had prophesied was the day that the Lord began His *Judgment of the dead* (in Heaven), and that Jesus would come to judge the living (on earth) after He finished judging the dead. As this was the center and heart of Adventist Theology, it was essential that she convince them that this was true. She spoke and they listened breathlessly, as she described how the Lord would come *soon*. She filled them with hope that would never be realized in their lifetime or in the lifetimes of those who have followed (till today). And still they believe and get more to believe in the Adventist philosophy that it will be very soon.

Ellen Harmon became *Ellen White*, the name she is known by, when she married James White, a pastor. She and her husband, along with Joseph Bates, Joshua Himes and Hiram Edson constituted the core of what became the Seventh Day Adventists. Her husband James later served as the president when it was established in Battle Creek, Michigan, with the help of Dr. Kellog, of Kellog Cereals.

Ellen White was *the* driving force behind the movement for many years, despite her handicap. She wrote forty-five books and more than 4,000 articles, with a third-grade education! Her book, *Steps to Christ* was translated into eighty-five languages and sold five million copies. All her books were based on her visions. Her husband said that she had more than 200 visions!

We're told that these books about her visions have exercised more of an influence on the growth of this sect than any other force. *That is scary!* Do you realize the influence this woman with her third grade education and her visions have had and continue to have on the world? They have always played a critical part in the strategy and structure of this sect, and they continue to be more of a motivating instrument in the life and multiplication of the sect than the Bible. These books play a major part in the escalating growth of the Seventh Day Adventists.

[Author's note: *We can really believe this last paragraph. Let us tell you why. This year, we gave a Lenten mission in Nampa, Idaho, about forty miles outside Boise. On the way back to the airport in Boise on Monday morning, we passed a huge complex of printing factories, on the side of the freeway, that seemed to go on forever. They were*

Seventh Day Adventist printing facilities. They were so large,
they were staggering.

If that wasn't enough, when we arrived at the Boise
airport, there were little kiosks with free magazines put out
by the Seventh Day Adventists in full color, slick and
obviously expensive to produce, free to anyone who was
travelling to or from Boise; inside the magazine was an offer
of a twelve month subscription at no charge. On the cover
was a picture of Billy Graham and an article on him inside
the magazine; if we didn't know better we would have thought
he was Adventist. Their most successful means of
proselytizing has been through the print media; they've now
added radio and television as other outreaches for their
ambition to make the world Adventist.]

Although they number more than 2,000,000 in the
world, most of their members live outside the United States.
Their greatest outreach has been and continues to be to
Hispanics in the United States; and, as with other sects and
cults, Mexico and South America - their *principle* avenue of
attack. Sadly, because these people have not been fed the
Truth, the Catholic Church with too few missionaries
evangelizing, this is where the Adventists and others, are
experiencing their greatest reception and success. Their
missionary effort is extremely successful, accounting for the
great number of converts to their religious group.

They are extremely organized. Each local church is
governed as a congregation, but they belong to a state
conference, which appoints a head. Four or more of these
conferences make up a union conference, and several union
conferences (more than five) make up a division. The world
is divided into *ten divisions* in 189 countries. Their world
headquarters is in Washington, D.C.

What do the Adventists believe?

The next time, someone suggests you join this philanthropic sect with their hospitals and schools, their willing aid to the downtrodden and lonely, ask them to tell you what *they* believe, not what *you* believe! Because they will betray you, casting stones at the Church Jesus founded, out of ignorance or design.

Beliefs

Doctrines uniquely theirs:

(a) They consider Saturday the Sabbath, not Sunday, as do all Christians.

(b) Unlike Christians, they do not believe that the soul is immortal. Instead they maintain that the soul is buried, along with the body. They also believe that only the just shall have eternal life, and that they will receive this immortality only when Jesus comes again.

(c) They observe the Kosher laws of the Old Testament coming from Deuteronomy and Leviticus where it is prescribed which foods are clean and which are unclean forbidding followers to eat food that is considered unclean, parts of the cow and most especially pork.

Their general beliefs are:

(a) Christ is coming to rebuild His Kingdom on earth;

(b) this Kingdom will last 1000 years;

(c) before His Second Coming, Christ will first purge the earth of the devil and his evil ones, all who do not belong to the Adventists and follow their dogmas.

They have taken from the Protestants *sola Scriptura* and follow this Fundamentalism, in that they believe:

(a) the Bible is the only authority on faith and morals;

(b) they believe in the Holy Trinity,

(c) and that Christ is Divine.

(d) They believe in *Justification by faith alone.*

(e) They follow the Ten Commandments.

✲ ✲ ✲

We have no problems with Seventh Day Adventists walking the road they have chosen to the Kingdom, and we do not judge the unusual way their organization has come about. But its not our walk and we do not want them or any other sect or cult taking Catholics away from Jesus and His Church. We have not written this to disparage them, but to inform Catholics what this sect believes and how they came to be. Then if they wish to join them, we only ask one thing: Remember Jesus said *He* is the Way, the Truth and the Life.

Footnotes

[1]in Bob & Penny Lord's *Trilogy Book II - Tragedy of the Reformation*

[2]This cult went by the name of *Heaven's Gate*, and you can read more about them in the chapter: *Save our Children*, in this book.

[3]where it had originated with William Miller

[4]Rev 14:8

[5]Rev 7:1-7

[6]Rev 7:4

[7]Gal 6:16

[8]Rev 14:1-5

[9]In Old Testament days the Dispersion (or Diaspora) meant the Jews who had emigrated from their country. James is referring to the Jewish-Christians who were now living in the Greek-Roman world.

[10]Jas1:1

Christian Scientists

Mary Baker Eddy

Mary Baker Eddy, foundress of the Christian Scientist movement, and Martin Luther would have had some go-round with each other. Luther preached that man was intrinsically evil and could do nothing to bring about his redemption, but that his fate had already been sealed before he was born, or predestination. Mary Baker Eddy believed just the opposite, that man was incapable of sin, sickness and death. Loyal followers of hers have followed this theology to the death, literally. There have been cases in the news over the past years of parents denying medical for themselves or their children for religious reasons. These, for the most part, would be followers of Mary Baker Eddy, the Christian Scientists.

In an age of Science, it seems a contradiction in terms that a religion using the term "Science" in its title, would disregard all scientific advances made in the last century and a half. And yet this is exactly what the Christian Scientists do. They deny the reality of disease, of matter, of evil and of death itself. Basically, if you get sick, just think positive thoughts and you will be healed. It would seem like mind over matter. Let us give you some background on this cult, which by the way, denies every fundamental Christian Doctrine that we believe, and yet subscribes to

Christianity and uses all Christian expressions.

It all began with Mary Baker Eddy, or to be more precise, Mary Baker Glover Patterson Eddy, having had three husbands. Her early life was fairly nondescript, other than that she was sick for most of it. She missed most of her formal education because of her illness. Here again, we have the founder of a major cult in the United States who had virtually no formal education. *And*, ironically enough, her followers include the cream of the literate society, including senators, an astronaut, college professors, movie stars, financiers and lawyers. Figure it out. Her lack of credentials ranks her with founders of many of our American sects or cults, as we prefer to call them, including Jehovah's Witnesses, Mormons and Seventh Day Adventists.

She married husband number one, George Washington Glover at an early age, 22, but the marriage only lasted six months as he died of yellow fever. She had her only child with George. His death caused her nervous situation to become worse. She began delving into *Mysticism, Mesmerism,* a form of hypnotism based on *Animal Magnetism,* and *Spiritualism.* All this was in an effort to relieve her of her physical ailments.

She married a Dr. Daniel Patterson who didn't help her physical problems either. He was a ladies' man and a dentist in that order. Her life with him was miserable. During this time, her physical and marital problems became worse. Her husband visited a Confederate battlefield as an observer and wound up in a Confederate prison in the south. Her son was taken to Minnesota and was brought up by foster parents for a reason not explained. Things were not going well. Her next move went from bad to worse.

She heard of a healer in Portland, Maine, whose name was Doctor Phineas P. Quimby. She went to him as a patient and student in 1862 and again in 1864. Apparently he did some good, because her praises of him in print were embarrassing to her followers. She was a devotee of the doctor until his death two years later in 1866. She gave him a tribute at his death which affirmed that she had been seriously influenced by him. However, after her death, those who followed either played down his importance in the role of the Christian Science movement, or eliminated him altogether.

The first claimed healing through Christian Science took place when Mary Baker slipped on the ice and suffered injuries which she maintained were uncurable. Her doctor did not necessarily agree with her. However, she went into Scripture and found healing messages which she claims the Early Church lost through abandonment of its principles. In reading the Bible, she found a passage in Matthew, *"Rise, pick up your stretcher and go home."*[1] According to her testimony, this gave her reason to believe that illness was not real, nor was death. Shortly after this realization, within days, she was able to get up and walk around. There is, however, a hitch. The doctor never agreed that her fall was not curable, that she was a hopeless case. As a matter of fact, he made up an affidavit to that effect.

That notwithstanding, Mary Baker Glover (she had resumed her first married name, shedding the name of the non-christian man to whom she had been married, and who had deserted her) plunged into her new realization and began writing feverishly. Within four years, she had written a textbook, called *"Science and Health With Key to the Scriptures."* It was by no means an overnight success. As a matter of fact, some of the reviews and comments on it were less than kind.

In later years, when she developed a following, the textbook received rave notices from those who supported her and her operation. And today, there are those who honor this book in their homes and in their lives with the same respect they might give to the writings of the Evangelists. But that is now and then was then. It took years before anyone even opened her book.

When she finally brought it out on the market five years later, she or someone promoted it in a way which would not be in keeping with the high level her organization demands today. It was like a hawker, or a peddler at a circus. The copy was as follows: *"A book that affords an opportunity to acquire a profession by which you can accumulate a fortune."* And this from a book with a title, *"Science and Health with a Key to Scriptures?"*

The years were not kind to Mary Baker. She found herself connected with a faith healer who gave himself the title "Doctor" just like Phineas Quimby. His name was Richard Kennedy. Together they promoted a lecture series on Christian Science. She gave a series of twelve lectures at a cost of $300. At first, she didn't think she would be able to get that kind of money in the industrial town of Lynn, Massachusetts; but she insisted the Lord had told her that was to be the price, and she charged it.

In her courses, she denied the reality of matter, evil sickness and death. She maintained that these were not from God, but man's errors from the mind. When dismissed, the suffering would disappear and death would be cheated. Man was not supposed to have to endure these sufferings through his life. All he had to do was apply the principles she espoused.

However, there was a flip side to this philosophy. She contended that if they could be used for purposes of health, they could also be misapplied to inflict sickness and death. We don't quite understand how this works, but she was convinced it would, and so were her followers. She called this misapplication or reversion of her teachings *Malicious*

Animal Magnetism, which was a form of Yankee voodooism, a revival of New England witchcraft. This haunted Mary Baker Eddy in later years. Malicious Animal Magnetism plagued her with evil thoughts brought on by her enemies and critics. For a time, she employed volunteers whose

Christian Science Monitor

sole job was to protect her from the evil forces present through Malicious Animal Magnetism.

For a time, there was a column in the Christian Science Journal in which fellow members of the Christian Science family shared experiences where they had been hexed by the same Malicious Animal Magnetism. This, however, has been eliminated from the Christian Science philosophy as a chapter in the history of the cult which was better off closed.

She married a third time, to Asa Gilbert Eddy who didn't live for very many years. Her Christian Science philosophy was not able to help him. However, Mary Baker Eddy insisted her husband died as a victim of Malicious Animal Magnetism. She stated: "My husband's death was caused by Malicious Animal Magnetism...I know it was poison that killed him, not material poison but mesmeric poison."

Her healing ministry caught on. Some of her students, encouraged by the exodus of "Doctor" Kennedy, the faith healer, began spreading out, founding their own cults. They were using her system without paying her royalties. This led to lawsuits and unpleasantries all around. Mrs. Eddy finally closed up shop in Lynn, Massachusetts and moved on to Boston. This is where the cult of Christian Science

First Church of Christ, Scientist in Massachusetts

really took off.

She was sixty-one years old when she moved her operation to Boston. She founded a church, which she called the *First Church of Christ, Scientist.* She got a charter for a college, the *Massachusetts Metaphysical College.* She was the only instructor. She was not about to have the problem she had encountered with "Doctor" Kennedy or the student rebellion in Lynn. Over a period of eight years, 4000 students went through the college at a cost of $300 per student.

At sixty eight years old, Mary Baker Eddy adopted a forty one year old man. He was a real doctor. It proved to be a poor choice for which she would pay in later years. She continued to live under the shadow of her real or imagined enemy of Malicious Animal Magnetism. She became restless with her college and closed it down. Why not? She was the only teacher. There was no one to pick up the slack. By now, she was seventy years old. She wanted to get out of Boston. She found a way to restructure her church in a way that she could have more control over it by centralizing the operation. She moved to an estate in Concord, Massachusetts, some seventy miles from Boston. But she ran her church with an iron grip until her death.

She ordained herself; she made herself Pastor Emeritus of her newly built church, the Mother Church, which was dedicated fifteen years before her death. But the last ten years of her life, she went downhill physically pretty quickly.

How she managed to cheat death for ten years was a major feat. Finally, in 1910, she gave her body up to Brother Death, though she never acknowledged his existence.

The saddest part of Mary Baker Eddy's life was that she died. She couldn't live the lie forever. Everything she had taught and believed in proved incorrect when she drew her last breath. She was so convinced that she would not die, she had made no provisions for a funeral. There is a clause in her Church Manual which states that nothing can be adopted, amended, or annulled without the written consent of the Leader, which is Mary Baker Eddy. Based on that, nothing can have happened since 1910.

Mary Baker Eddy gave in to the error of mortal mind. She did what she said could not happen. Man's purpose in life is to free himself from these errors of mortal mind through application of the laws she had discovered. Once freed, he would find himself healthy, sinless and immortal. What happened to Mary Baker Eddy? Did she finally lose the battle to the Malicious Animal Magnetism, or was she just wrong?

✳ ✳ ✳

We have a personal testimony. Our Penny Lord, when she was in college, was in a production of "The Heiress" in which she played the lead. During the rehearsal of that play, our son Richard got the mumps. Now this is a very normal thing for a young boy. The mumps are a very uncomfortable affliction for children; they are horrendous for adults. Penny, being the super mom she has always been, stayed with her son in the same room, hugging him, loving him and trying to take away the mumps.

The evening of the dress rehearsal for the play came. They wore bonnets in that play. As the dress rehearsal progressed, Penny's bonnet, which had fit very well all during the dress rehearsal, began to feel extremely tight.

She went to the director and told her that her face seemed to be swelling up. The director was a Christian Scientist. She told Penny to think good thoughts, and to pray. The discomfort would go away. Penny took her advice and began to pray. The swelling got so bad she had to remove the bonnet. Now the costume was becoming too tight. Bob brought Penny home.

We continued to think good thoughts for the rest of the night. Penny became larger and larger, swelling more and more until she had no shape. She looked like an egg. The pain was excruciating. Needless to say, Bob removed himself from the proximity of Penny, because if you think mumps are mean for kids to have, and really bad for a mom to catch, you don't even want to imagine what they would be like for a man. Penny didn't play in the production. When she returned after the mumps were gone, the director told her she didn't have enough faith. *I don't think that was the reason.*

✻ ✻ ✻

Christian Scientists don't take medicine, or confer with physicians. However, they are allowed to go to obstetricians, dentists, eye doctors and undertakers. That last one is a little strange seeing as how they don't accept mortal death.

Christian Scientists are basically a self-help group. Their philosophy is much like what Penny's director advised up above. The results, however, more than not, turn out like Penny's.

There have been cures attributed to the kind of mental medicine prescribed by Mary Baker Eddy and her followers. However, those scientists who give credit to the mind for healing the body explain it somewhat differently than the Christian Scientists. They do believe there is illness and they do believe there is death. Many doctors today will agree that the mind can heal or kill. Some members of the

Psychology and Psychiatry community deny the existence of sin, having renamed what Christians call sin, neuroses. Psychology and Psychiatry are admittedly not exact sciences. But with that exception, the medical community doesn't deny the reality of sickness, sin and death.

An interesting point has to be made. While Christian Scientists are encouraged to self-help, or heal themselves, they do have a staff of Christian Scientists who are, *guess what?* healers and practitioners, much like the Christian world's doctors. They have offices and office hours, and you have to pay them for sure. They are listed in a directory somewhat like the American Medical Association's directory, only they're Christian Scientist associates. They will treat non-Christian Scientists, but their methods are the same for any patient who comes to them. They try to talk the patient out of believing that they're sick or dying. They read to them from the Bible and *Science and Health with Key to the Scriptures*.

They have no facilities in their religion for Marriage ceremonies. They don't bury through the Christian Science church because they don't believe in death.

They recommend their people stay away from the exotic sins, like tobacco, alcohol, stimulants like tea or coffee, and definitely no drugs.

They reject all main teachings of Christianity, such as:
Personal God - they believe in a Pantheistic God.[2]
The Trinity
Sin, Original and Actual
Divinity of Christ
the existence of the devil
Baptism
Resurrection and atonement for sin
(because sin doesn't exist)
Heaven, Hell and for sure Purgatory

Holy Days such as Christmas and Easter

And it goes on and on.

We're warned not to confuse their use of Christian terms. As with many cults, such as Jehovah's Witnesses and Mormons, their meaning of these terms are not the same as ours. Their interpretation of Scripture is not the same as ours.

While they build, or at least during their heyday they did build huge temples, they never became involved in public service institutions such as hospitals, orphanages, welfare agencies or the like. They claim that to do so would be to cater to mortal error.

Christian Science is accepted mostly in larger metropolitan areas. Their members are a cut above the average intellectually. While their membership is very limited, they have been able to count as members, big names in politics and the arts. This becomes worrisome in light of the bizarre nature of their beliefs.

Christian Science is a hard religion to accept. It defies logic and common sense. Most potential converts can't get over the hurdle of no sickness, no death, no doctors. Chicken Pox, Mumps, Doctors, Hospitals, HMO's and eventually Brother Death are as American as Mom and apple pie. You don't take those things away.

The Christian Science Monitor, a daily newspaper, has been in existence since the time of Mary Baker Eddy. It's basically a public service institution with only one article directly involving Christian Science. However, you must understand that there is no such thing as subjective journalism. As hard as any ethical editor might try, none of us can help but bring our own agenda to whatever we write.

They say it is a financial drain on the Christian Science organization, which may be so. But it has won six Pulitzer Prizes for Journalism which is significant, especially since the rumors are that the reason Mary Baker Eddy began the newspaper in the first place was in response to a major attack on her personally by Joseph Pulitzer.

Membership has declined in the Christian Science movement since 1926. It had to. Her concept of life everlasting on this earth has completely fallen apart. Even though her Wednesday evening services are totally dedicated to word-of-mouth witnessing of healings, all those who were alive at the time of Mrs. Eddy are dead now, with possible exception of a handful. We can't credit lack of faith to all these people, because Mrs. Eddy is one of them who died.

It was an impossible notion that was fine as long as everyone was alive and well. But Brother Death has to come to visit. And when the truck backs up.....There are literally thousands of Scripture passages concerning "Death" "Dead" "Die" "Dying," but the one we believe which applies most to this situation is from Genesis when God spoke to Adam:

"In the sweat of your face
you shall eat bread
till you return to the ground,
for out of it you were taken;
you are dust,
and to dust you shall return."[3]

Footnotes

[1] Mt 9:6
[2] God is in the trees and in the air and in the water
[3] Gen 3:19

Fundamentalism

"There is a God!"

They say when you get older, you start to look back. Well we do not know how true that is, but one thing we can say, reflecting on our lives, seeing how the Lord has carefully guided the steps we have taken, blocking the wrong doors we could have opened, picking us up when we have fallen, and healing us when we were wounded, we know that He has always been with us, beside us, loving us! Just thinking of all that has come to pass in our lives, in our Ministry, in the life of the Church fills us with praise and thanksgiving to a faithful God Who has always watched over us.

When my niece (and godchild) heard we had given up our lives to follow Jesus by bringing the Catholic Church to the whole world, she said *"Aunt Penny you and Uncle Bob have always been religious."* I don't think that is quite the whole truth. You have to *know* your Faith to be religious; we loved Jesus and our Church, but with the *knowledge* of a child, not the *faith* of a child which Jesus asks us to have. And so, on our long journey to where Jesus wanted us, but for the Grace of God we could have fallen at any time. This is one of the reasons we do not condemn or criticize any brothers and sisters who have left the Catholic Church for whatever reason; it could have been us. This is why I am sharing some of the early experiences I had with some brothers and sisters in Christ, before we get into bringing you the Sect - Fundamentalism.

We are telling you about our mistakes and the tools that are being used to recruit Catholics and Protestants into sects, denominations, and cults so that you are aware and prayerfully the Holy Spirit can work through these books and keep you from falling. We love you. Our Church needs you. If there is one fault we see in our churches, because we have so many parishioners, we cannot reach out to all the workers who are just waiting to be asked to work in God's Vineyard - *The Catholic Church*. Be like us; volunteer! And if someone says they do not need you, call us, we need you!

"Have you been saved?" I remember the first time I heard that. We were still in the world, but I have always had a love affair going with Jesus. I was working with this distributor who was going to represent and distribute a line of merchandise that we manufactured. We had been negotiating and I was telling him all about our line, when he asked me if I was saved. I really didn't know what he was talking about, and when that seemed quite apparent, he said that I was to get down on my knees and accept Jesus as my personal Savior. He witnessed to me how he had been a bum, an alcoholic, stayed out to all hours of the night, and on and on; and then he found Jesus! It sounded great, but since Bob wasn't with me, I thought I'd better wait for him. P.S. The end of that story is that young man took our company for thousands of dollars, but that was nothing compared to the hundreds of thousands he absconded from other manufacturers bigger than Bob and me. *That was one!*

Then we became manufacturers representatives of gift items. As much of our gift items were country store type merchandise, the merchants were mainly *Born-Again Christians!* Most were very friendly; we loved Jesus and they did, too, so we had something in common. There was one buyer; we never had a chance to talk much about anything with her; she was strictly business, and furthermore she seemed as if she really did not like us much. Bob was going to work with her one day and arrived before she did. Now we had a station wagon with license plates reading RP LORD (meaning Robert and Penny Lord or, as she thought,

Our Precious Lord) and the license plate holder read "Jesus loves you." When she entered the store, the first thing she said to Bob was *"I didn't know that you were Christian."* From that time on, she was as sweet as apple pie. Wow! We had always run our business in a very Christian manner, and had always been loving to this buyer. It's sad that she did not consider us Christians until she saw our license plate holder. *That's two!*

Then there was this couple from somewhere in Northern California. The wife was the buyer of her store, and she too was not very friendly. We were getting ready for a major Gift Show and were redoing our showroom, when the wife came into the showroom. Upon seeing us working, she pitched in; I felt real good, as this was the first sign of friendship I had ever seen in her. She asked us about our trip to Europe. Excitedly, I began to tell her about the Shrines, most specially about those of Mother Mary. She seemed to be enjoying what we were telling her. Her husband came to bring her to lunch. I was feeling so good that we had shared with her, until she returned to the showroom from lunch, and this is what she said: *"We buy from you and what you sell is good, but we have religious differences that divide us, so I think it is better if we do not talk religion again."* I was speechless, I was so hurt!

Then a couple of weeks later, we were at Mass and I don't remember what the Scripture passage in the readings was, all I know is that Bob said we have to drive out to see these people, without our samples, just to say that we love them, we are one family and the Lord loves us all. We went about 150 miles to their store. When we arrived, they asked us where our samples were, and we explained we just wanted to take them out to lunch; we had not brought our samples. Lunch was progressing peacefully, when Bob told them we just wanted them to know we loved them. The woman whipped out her Bible and began attacking the Catholic Church, using Chapter and Verse. Bob and I did not know much Chapter and Verse, at the time. But an amazing thing happened, Bob was quoting Chapter and Verse defending the Faith. I knew it couldn't be him; it had to be the Holy Spirit. And all of a sudden I heard him say: *"You will not use the Word as a sword against My people."* As we were leaving, the wife said, *"It is so enlightening to find Catholics who know Scripture."* And that's three!

Then there was the woman who wanted to rip the crucifix off my neck, and who also insisted the woman who worked for us was going to hell, all because she was Jewish. She *demanded* we have the Jewish woman accept Jesus as her personal savior right there and then.

Now I am in no way saying that is what Fundamentalists do or who they are. I'm just sharing a very few of the experiences I have had that have left me a little more than disenchanted. Now, in no way are we inferring the Fundamental Churches are in the destructive class as cults like mind-altering, spiritualist, Hindu base New Age cults. We would just like to share the focus of Fundamentalists, and the way they go about recruiting for their churches, which makes them dangerous. You may be wondering why we have placed them in this book rather than in the book on the Reformation. Although the Reformation certainly influenced their theology and hate for the Catholic Church, *(though not all Fundamentalist spread hate against the Church, but all do preach against what we believe, with many spreading accusations and calling names unworthy of Christians, like the Pope being the anti-Christ and Catholics worshiping Mary)*, they are not part of the Main-Line Protestant religions, but one of the thousands of churches that have sprung up in the 20th Century. They are considered a sect because they preach *exclusivity* and proselytize by *belittling* other Faiths.

Often the most zealous outspoken Fundamentalists and recruiters are fallen-away Catholics who left the Church for one reason or another, but basically never knew the Church. The Fundamentalists love having fallen-away Catholics in their churches; in this way these brothers and sisters can be a sign that our Church is corrupt and this Fundamental church is the true church. Couple that with the misinformation these fallen-away Catholics bring to the Fundamentalists to use against the Catholic Church and you have some heavy proselytizing going on. Have you ever heard Fundamentalists say what they believe, except that they believe in the sole authority of the Bible? When you respond asking them if this is true and the Holy Spirit guides each person to interpret the Bible for himself, how come there are so many splinter cults and sects cropping up (as much as 5 per week in the United States alone, not counting little independent churches)? Are they suggesting the Holy Spirit is spreading confusion? Would He tell one person or persons one thing and others something else? God is not the God of confusion; Satan is the *father* of confusion. Have they ever said anything but quote Chapter and Verse to prove our Church is the *Whore of Babylon* and our dear Pope - the devil himself, to attack Mother Mary and all the Treasures of the Church we revere? They do not stop with the Catholic Church; their mode of recruiting encompasses attacks on Main-Line Protestant religions, but Catholicism is the main target.

How did Fundamentalism get going? As we have said, and we repeat, *There is no revolution without a cause.* At the end of the 19th Century, liberalism was slithering from under the stones and was rearing its ugly prideful head, infiltrating our churches - Catholics and Main-Line Protestant. Then in the beginning of the 20th Century, the

Catholic response was: Pope St. Pius X fought Modernism (or liberalism) by condemning it with an encyclical and by requiring all priests to take the Loyalty Oath. But sadly, the Word of God, little by little, was more and more *maltreated* on the altars, with men of God questioning the authenticity of Scripture, saying things like: *Jesus did not say this; the Gospel writers put these words in His Mouth to teach a certain people at a certain time in history*, going down-hill from there. People were upset and rightly so; they wanted to hear the Word of God extolled.

The birth of Fundamentalism!

The modernists were trying to destroy all that is supernatural, blasting the Bible as just a collection of so many stories. When people heard that there was a preacher who was reverently preaching the Word of God, hungry for that Word they flocked to his church. Fundamentalism was born out of protest against Catholic and Protestant liberalism!

The faithful who remained, began to fear the Word was being ripped apart, thread by thread, until eventually nothing would be left but a heap of meaningless empty words. All they could hear was the Word being dissipated and God's message to His children destroyed. Consequently, as a defense against Modernism, Fundamentalism came into being at the beginning of the 20th Century.

Universities and seminaries were being inundated by theologians spouting new old heresies, attacking the Word of God among other Truths. The *"Bible belt"* Midwest and South reacted by having Revivals and Bible conferences. It was at one of these Conferences that five points outlining a strictly conservative form of Fundamentalism came into fruition: (1) the inerrancy of the Bible; (2) Jesus is Divine; (3) the Virgin Birth; (4) Christ's Atonement for our sins; (5) Christ's *physical* Resurrection and future *physical* return.

Two wealthy laymen from Los Angeles published a

series of 12 small books called: *The Fundamentals: A Testimony to the Truth,* defending the Word and all its tenets. More and more articles appeared and magazines were printed, disseminating the word to all who hungered that the Bible and the Word of the Lord was real, and alive! By the 1920's this strong movement was being firmly entrenched in Protestant churches with the Presbyterians, the Methodists, the Baptists and the Disciples of Christ splitting into 3 different camps - Modernist, Fundamentalist and somewhere in-between. Lutherans and Episcopalians firmly rooted in their Faiths were not caught up in *this* revolution!

New orthodox Protestant seminaries started to open. So that which started as a very simplistic type of holding fast to the Word, bloomed into a spreading movement attracting professors and distinguished Protestant theologians. From 1914 until around 1940, the movement flourished and grew, although surrounded by much controversy: for example the court battle over Evolution. Although Fundamentalism has waned as a movement in recent years, it has become firmly assimilated into main-stream society, with its concepts influencing Protestants and many Catholics.

What are the dangers of the Fundamentalist Movement?

To begin with, little churches are formed with pastors doing little more than preaching and operating the church. The congregation hires and fires the pastor. If he is not preaching according to what they want to hear, anyone in the church can disagree with him. For this reason, many bring Bibles to church, looking up passages while the pastor is preaching, to check up on him and verify his sermon. A disagreement in interpretation could get him fired, if they don't like him; or if he has firmly been accepted by the elders, the differences might be settled by the pastor suggesting if the person or persons don't like his preaching, maybe they would be better off in some other church.

Very often the pastor interprets the Word according to his own personal opinion, untrained and unskilled in theology though he may be, leading his flock to another splinter even farther away from the Truth of the True Cross of Christ. Many come from very simple backgrounds, (like one where we formerly lived who had been a gardener when he began a church) their education having nothing to do with knowledge of the Bible. With this free-for-all type of theology, the little church finds itself splitting into another schism. Very few stay in one little church more than a year. Becoming disenchanted with this or that, maybe the preacher they loved is no longer there, or they do not get along with the *new* people who have joined the congregation, off they go *church-shopping.*

As we said before, the most deadly proselytizers are fallen-away Catholics. I went to the same hair stylist (I think that's what they want to be called) for about 13 years. I was very fond of her and she was very fond of me. We only had one problem; she was away from the Church and she was convinced Bob and I should be with her in *her* church. So every time I was with her, she would spend our time together trying to talk me into joining her church. This one day, I asked her if she thought I was happy. She said yes, and that's why I belonged in her church. Then I added, did she think I was filled with the Holy Spirit; again yes and the same reasoning - I belonged in her church. Finally I said, *"You say I am happy and I am filled with the Holy Spirit, why would I join your church; you are always knocking my Church and I have never seen you happy?"*

She always told me about the pastor and the great congregation in the Four Square Church. Then one day, she began telling me about the great choir, and how she had joined Calvary Community Church. I asked her what happened to the other church that was so great, I just had to join. *"Well,"* she answered, *"they merged with this other pastor and his congregation and it's not the same. This church is different; the music is great and they put on the greatest pageants every Easter and Christmas. Why don't you join us on Sundays? Many Catholics come to Calvary and still go to the Catholic Church."* I wanted to ask her how many Catholics who go there are still Catholics, but I knew it was to no avail. The last time I saw her she was not going to any church.

The sad thing is she is not the exception. The Fundamentalist churches are mainly *horizontal*, people churches. You may recall, the first thing Cranmer did, (the Calvinist, who took over the Church of England), was take the altars off the Sanctuary and place them within the congregation, in the middle so that the people would face one another. With the *"decent table"* (as they now called their altars), in the middle of the congregation, they really were not focusing on the Eucharist,[1] nor on the Word, but on each other. And as with my little friend, the hair stylist, when you find your neighbors in church distasteful, what do you do, leave the church and go church shopping. And then when your heart still yearns for He Whom you have left, Jesus in the Eucharist, do you go from church to church to agnosticism and finally no church?

Although we thank the Fundamentalists of the early Twentieth Century for their relentless fight against Modernism and the adulteration of the Word, we must in all conscience remind them that the Bible they use was altered and stripped of books in the 16th Century. We must ask them to remember that it was the *Catholic Church* that chose the books of the Bible, that they so wrongfully and often mercilessly use against us, wounding us. It is an established fact that Fundamentalists are so absorbed with promoting their religious doctrines, they have made their beliefs the end, rather than a means to an end.

Love your brothers and sisters who are Fundamentalists!

Love them with the Immaculate Heart of Mary, perfect Mother who loves all her children, even those who have left home and attack her, and the compassionate Sacred Heart of Jesus Who died for all. But do not condone what they teach or the methods they use. *Ecumenism* is not the Catholic Church giving up Truths which have transcended 2000 years, but for those who are separated from the True Church to come Home, the Arms of Jesus and Mary open wide to accept them.

We just returned from a glorious Catholic Conference where we met a former Baptist minister and his wife who had converted to the Catholic Church. I wish I could share with you the light that came from their eyes when they spoke of Mother Church and the Lord Who dwells within in the Eucharist. Pastor Goebel began to cry when he explained that it was Mother Mary who had called them Home to the Catholic Church. Their daughter-in-law was with them. Although baptized Catholic, she had left the Church and because of what she and her husband saw in her in-laws, she and he were studying the Faith, preparing to enter, as well. This chapter is for them, for Marcus and Marilyn Grodi[2] and for the many former Protestants, ministers, wives and laity who are now a light in our Church.

Footnotes

[1] as they no longer had the Eucharist, the true presence of Jesus, Body, Blood, Soul and Divinity

[2] convert who was formerly a minister and now has a Series on EWTN called: *The Journey Home*, where converts, especially former ministers appear and tell their conversion story.

Televangelism

The Electronic Church

Who is that you have invited into your living room?

Evangelists

Before the birth of television, the nightly and Sunday pastime was sitting before the radio, listening intently to everything from *The Shadow* to Helen Hayes on the Mercury Theater, to listening to Mama and Papa, their ears glued to the little box, reporting what little *news* they could gather on how our brother and other boys were doing overseas, fighting in World War II. We didn't move; we were mesmerized. Then there was Archbishop Fulton J. Sheen with his dynamic booming passionate voice bringing us Jesus. But he was not the only voice bringing Jesus. There were also false prophets crowding the air waves.

Aimee Semple McPherson

Aimee Semple McPherson, originally Aimee Semple Kennedy, was born in 1890 in Canada, near Ingersoll, Ontario. Her father was a Methodist farmer and a Salvation Army worker. Aimee met Robert Semple, an evangelist and married him in 1908. She joined him, working in a mission in Hong Kong. Their work was to be cut short when he died there in 1910. She returned to the United States where she met Harold McPherson whom she married in 1912. This did not last long; she left him to begin her career - preaching and faith healing! Aimee started the *International Church of the Foursquare Gospel*. She was quite successful and the generous donations that kept on rolling in allowed her to open *The Angelus Temple* in Los Angeles. For the next 20 years, she would fill the 5000 seats of this temple with people seeking miracles and those desiring sensationalism. She was a showman *par excellence*, healing and preaching, her main theme: the Four roles of *Jesus Christ: Healer, Baptizer, Savior*, and His *Second Coming as King*. One thing leading to another, she was able to establish a radio station, found a Bible School and edit a magazine.

One of the early radio preachers, I can still remember hearing my parents speaking about her and her wild missions and tent revivals. They would hear her on the radio, see her on the movie screen when the news came on before the movie, in the local theater. They thought it was all a scam and never believed she was healing the people who were crying out they were healed. To them, she was just like other *holy rollers* (that's what Pentecostals were called, in those days) that we would hear on the radio, clapping their hands calling out during the service, singing spirituals never heard in St. Joseph's Catholic Church.

But as all things eventually will be led from out of the darkness into the light, scandal befell Aimee. In May, 1926, there was news of her drowning in the Pacific Ocean. Then five weeks later, she reappeared, with the story she had been kidnapped and held for ransom. She was accused of perjury and brought to trial. There was not enough evidence and she was acquitted. This did not greatly affect her. She continued her preaching almost to the day she died in 1951. It's amazing how some questionable people bounce back, and some very holy people die in disgrace later to be exonerated and declared Saints.

Televangelists

It is amazing. Whereas most Catholics would not think of going to a church other than the Roman Catholic Church, and listen to a Preacher who was not teaching according to the Magisterium of the Church, Televangelists report that conservatively 40% of their contributors and viewers are Catholic. Now, although there are some fine Televangelists, they are not preaching the fullness of Truth that is found in the Catholic Church.

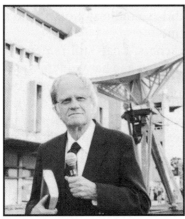

Billy Graham

1918 - Billy Graham

Born William Franklin Graham, Billy Graham is possibly the best known and most authentic of the Televangelists, as well as lead spokesman for Fundamentalism. He has been the friend and spiritual advisor to many Presidents from Harry Truman to Bill Clinton. He has the distinction of having received the Congressional Gold Medal.

Billy Graham was born in Charlotte, North Carolina in 1918, went to Bob Jones University, the Florida Bible Institute, and Wheaton College. He was ordained in the Southern Baptist Church in 1939, and became pastor of the First Baptist Church of Western Springs, Illinois in 1943. In 1949, he catapulted into a world-wide career of evangelization, combing first our country, then Europe, and then the whole world.

Because of his universal appeal, and his powerful presentations, he fills stadiums with hundred of thousands of people. These rallies are all televised and have made him a household name. Billy Graham is famous for his *"altar calls"* where you see people, especially young men and women streaming up to the stage to accept Jesus as their personal Savior. He has great access to living rooms all over the United States because, as he is considered *non-denominational*,[1] he appeals to Protestants of all denominations as well as Catholic viewers. Unlike some of his brother Televangelists, he does not preach a sermon of hate and criticism of other Faiths, in particular the Catholic Faith.

He has influenced many through his very own motion pictures, his magazine *"Decision"* which is produced by the Billy Graham Evangelistic Association, through his radio program - *The Hour of Decision*, a syndicated column, and through his books: *Peace with God* which he wrote in 1953, *Secret of Happiness* in 1955, *My Answer* in 1960, *World Aflame* in 1965 and *How to be born again* in 1977.

When asked what brings him the most happiness, he replied: *"To stand up and proclaim the gospel of Christ. And to step down from the pulpit and know that I have not compromised, and that I've been faithful to what God has called me to do."*

Billy Graham has been faithful to what God has asked of him - where God planted him; but for Catholics to be learning about the Bible, even from a good man like Billy Graham, is leaving themselves open to error, because although he is sincere in what he teaches, it is not the whole Truth as revealed through the Catholic Church.[2]

Do I believe that Billy Graham is a good man? Yes and it would appear that he and our Pope John Paul II certainly have a mutual high regard for one another, as evidenced by the friendship plainly visible between the two, when the Pope gave Billy Graham an audience. This is the unity our Lord spoke of; here were two brothers in Christ, with differing beliefs talking together, respecting each other and their differences.

But the Pope and Billy Graham did not worship together. It was like when the Pope met with all the heads of the different churches of the world, including even Moslems, Buddhists, and Hindus, he said "We can pray together but we cannot worship together." And we add *yet*, Billy Graham; for if you delve one more step closer to the best kept secret in the world, the Treasure we have in our Church - the Eucharist, maybe like your fellow ministers who have come Home to Rome, we will see you in our Church, before we go Home to Jesus. We love you and respect you.

Oral Roberts

Born in Oklahoma, Oral Roberts was ordained by the Pentecostal Holiness Church, like his father before him. He began preaching at revivals and healing services in tents, grew to radio and then to television. He founded *Oral Roberts University* and *City of Faith Medical Center*. He pushes miraculous healings, allegedly brought about through him, in his publication *Abundant Life*. He has made the front page, the enemy always ready and anxious to cast mud on someone espousing Jesus, with his statement that Jesus was going to take him home, if he didn't get eight million dollars.

This is the kind of televangelism, with which there is a problem. We do not wish to question his motives or whether he really believes that Jesus said this to him. But this is not how we envision Jesus. This we're *King's kids* and *the Lord wants us to be rich, no cross, no suffering* philosophy is not the Lord and the Way He chose for Himself. Reading the lives of the Saints and those now who are serving Him, the Way is through the Cross, with never quite enough, the work much and the workers few - the Way of the Cross!

Jimmy Swaggart

A home-grown evangelist, in 1935, Jimmy Lee Swaggart came into the world with a promise of evangelizing the Word of God. Born in Ferriday, Louisiana, Swaggart grew up in a small town near Natchez, Mississippi. His family always involved in the Assemblies of God, his uncle paid for the erection of an Assemblies of God Church in Natchez. He did not get his yearning to be a preacher from out of the blue; both his parents were evangelists and he grew up hearing his grandmother quoting the Bible. As we have said at talks and conferences, grandparents play such a key role in the spiritual upbringing of the child, if they are not locked away in some Retirement Home. It was his grandmother who was with him, having brought him to a Prayer Meeting, when the nine year old Jimmy felt the call to ministry.

But as children are sometimes like the seed which fell among thorns and the thorns grew up and choked it,[3] the world and its temptations soon kept the boy Jimmy busy playing the piano and singing with his cousin Jerry Lee Lewis (who would grow up to become one of Rock and Roll's early legends). But the time would shortly come when Jimmy Swaggart would use his knowledge of music to help him, when he began preaching on street corners. It also opened doors for him in churches because he would lead the congregation singing and accompany them on the piano or his accordion.

He became a full-fledged preacher in 1958. Not content to reach those few, he began recording gospel record albums, with the target - exposure on *Christian radio stations*. Revival meetings always having been the rage in the Bible belt South, Jimmy was to gain quite a reputation preaching in one town after the other, wherever there was a Revival Meeting, which was in practically every small hamlet. 1969 came and Swaggart was able to air his new radio program *"The Camp Meeting Hour"* on hundreds of radio stations.

Television took over from radio and *evangelist* Jimmy

Swaggart became *televangelist* Jimmy Swaggart in 1973. Within 10 years, he became one of the most popular of the Protestant television preachers. His program, *"The Jimmy Swaggart Telecast"* was carried by 200 stations, reaching 2,000,000 homes.[4] His ministry now located in Baton Rouge, Louisiana included a congregation of 4000 members, a Bible College, a plant which printed his literature that was then sown among his faithful listeners of radio and viewers of T.V. (many who were Catholic), a building which produced his television shows, and a high-tech recording studio.

He is known for his extremely theatrical presentation of Fundamentalism on television, sparing no one, Protestant and Catholic alike; but like some other televangelists, he attacks the Catholic Church the most bitterly, taking nasty pot-shots at all we believe and treasure in our Faith. Not satisfied to call the Church foul names, using Scripture to justify himself, he spares no one, damning Pope John Paul II and Mother Teresa equally. And yet, over the years poor innocent, uninformed Catholics have financed his program with their hard-earned contributions.

What does Swaggart preach beside hate against other churches, his fundamental message is total and *literal belief in the Bible* (which he manipulates to suit one of his particular harangues, justify his actions, or demand for money); he speaks to an enthralled audience incessantly of *"miraculous healings."* Part of his outreach to Pentecostals is his preaching on *"speaking in tongues"* and his ongoing message that Jesus is coming soon. He has always followed the Protestant line of: *If you accept Jesus as your personal Savior you are saved.* His histrionics included tirades on *hell, fire and brimstone*, damning this and that one, to the point of broadcasting the unfortunate scandal of famous televangelists, Jim and Tammy Bakker. Although the Bakkers were found guilty of wrong-doing, the way

Swaggart, a supposed brother in Christ, used this fall from Grace to destroy them was hardly Christian. He employed the power he had in his vast communication outreaches, in particular television, to scandalize and crucify them.

But what goes around, comes around, Swaggart was to fall from Grace. The mercy and understanding he did not show the Bakkers, he tearfully begged from his viewers, many of whom forgave him. The crazy justification he used for his sins was that as a man of God he had certain needs other men are not privy to. Swaggart got caught in a series of compromising situations with prostitutes which almost ruined his career. Tears running down his cheeks, he told his television audience that he had thought of stepping down, but the Lord told him he must go on, he must endure the slings and arrows of his enemies. He was referring to his being chastised by the Assemblies of God Church for his sexual misconduct which made all the papers and television news media. Swaggart separated from the Assemblies of God Church and like so many before him, went his own way!

✳ ✳ ✳

We have chosen just a small sampling of the many televangelists coming into your living rooms, to give you contrasts and similarities, smatterings of truth mixed with error, a warning to adore and revere the Treasures you have in the Catholic Church and bloom where you are planted!

In keeping with the aims and charism of our Roman Catholic Church, our Ministry has defended the Church not by attacking, but rather by speaking and writing the truth! When a church uses one of God's gift (as in the case of the Fundamentalist's use of Scripture), to hurt another Church (the Catholic Church) attacking God's gifts to them, this denomination or sect and their work cannot be blessed.

We entreat our brothers and sisters to remember Jesus' words that we love one another. We *all* want to serve God.

We *all* desire to glorify Jesus' Name. We *all* love the Lord. We have *all* taken different paths, and we do not judge you. We can and will pray for you, but we will not compromise Jesus and all He has left for us to do, by denying the Church and any part of that which she teaches. We are the Church He founded upon the Rock who is Peter - our first Pope, and all the Popes who have come after him. When Jesus' Heart was pierced out of love for us, our Church flowed from that precious Side. When you attack that Church you attack Jesus' Mystical Body, you attack Him. We love you. Let not pettiness and past hurts keep us apart. *Come Home!*

Footnotes

[1]that is a misnomer as those who are non-denominational teach *their* own concepts of what *they* believe the Scriptures are saying.

[2]Want to bring Christ into your living room, turn on Mother Angelica, Eternal Word Television Network.

[3]Mk 4:7

[4]EWTN Television is the world's largest religious cable network reaching 54 million homes in 34 countries and 4 territories twenty-four hours a day. EWTN Radio broadcasts twenty-four hours a day, via WEWN Shortwave to a potential listening audience of over 700 million around the world. Using the satellite reach of EWTN Television, the AM/FM Radio service is transmitted to over 18 million AM/FM listeners. EWTN Online Services provides Catholic information, and resource documents, and audio from EWTN Radio live twenty-four hours a day, 365 day a year to anyone with Internet access. Today, over 30 million worldwide Internet users can access EWTN's web site at http://www.ewtn.com, and find an extensive profile of all EWTN's services -- daily news, reports, television highlights, novenas, or live radio programs.

Save our children

"Whoever causes one of these little one to sin....."

There is a madness spreading throughout the world with a well-planned, well-disguised design; its tentacles are snatching our children and devouring them. There are cults and cults. The world is telling parents to let go, untie the apron strings, only to find their children helplessly bound to a *new* family and a guru who dominates their every thought and action. What makes young men and women leave all they have held dear, turn their backs on family, parents, wives, siblings, and children? There are thousands of cults. Allow us to share some of the most deadly in one way or the other. We will begin with a recent cult that has surfaced from beneath the slithering enemy's pile of slippery stones.

✳

Marshall Herff Applewhite

Heaven's Gate

We have been hearing from different parts of the world that whole cults have committed mass suicides. The one most tragic and close to home was that of the senseless deaths of members of a cult called *Heaven's Gate*. It was one of the worst mass suicides in the history of our nation, coming close to Jim Jones' senseless slaughter of 914 followers in Jonestown in 1978. Heaven's Gate founder *Marshall Herff Applewhite* had been declared mentally ill at one time in his life, had been accused of homosexual misconduct with a student and dismissed from the university where he taught; all of which he did not deny. Instead, he openly admitted he castrated himself to fight his homosexual urges. He was even able to convince other men in his cult to do the same, in the name of chastity.

Couples left their children, some as young as new born twins. Mothers brought their daughters to the cult, believing this was a brave new world Marshall Herff Applewhite and his co-conspirator Bonnie Nettles were offering them. Little did these idealists, seeking the Kingdom, know when they said their first *yes* that it would lead them on a journey to death. They were seduced into believing they were on their way to the Father in Heaven. Applewhite, like so many cult leaders, touched upon an inner desire they had to be closer to God. After a short while he became their god. Thirty-nine of Jesus' lambs trusted these false prophets and went to their death.

A computer programmer, age 43, told his girlfriend: "I want to join my heavenly Father and my classmates."

Most of those who took their lives appeared to be very ordinary citizens - all searching for more spirituality; and judging they could not find it in this world, sought a new world. When a mother of one of the women who had solved her disenchantment with this world by joining in this mass suicide, heard about her daughter's death, she replied: "The way to change the world is not to leave it."

We are in serious times, very serious times! Our Lord, in His Word warns us:

"For false Christs and false prophets will arise and show great signs and wonders, so as to lead astray, if possible, even the elect."[1]

And then St. Paul in the First Century warns us about cults when he addresses the Colossians:

"See to it that no one deceive you through any empty, seductive philosophy that follows based on cosmic powers

rather than on Christ. "[2]

What was their new world like? Applewhite trained his followers to go out and proselytize; but quite clandestinely, as he did not want their families to find their lost loved ones who seemed to have disappeared from the face of the earth. He ran the cult like a strict military encampment. He always insisted each member be accompanied by another member, whether eating, sleeping or out gathering more followers. He changed partners of the members frequently, lest one become attracted to the other. He even had them wear loose clothes to disguise their sexual differences. He espoused a philosophy reminiscent of age-old heresies that called the body evil. Although thirty-nine died, it seems inconceivable that at one time there were hundreds who belonged to this movement where all personal liberty was relinquished at the command of a certifiable mad man.

For ten years he kept predicting the landing of a space ship that would bring them up to Heaven. Wouldn't you think after ten years of futile expectations unfulfilled, they would have had a clue he was not heavenly inspired, but instead seriously deluded? We have researched cults that followed a similar pattern, their founders predicting the very day the world would end; and the baffling truth is these cults have followers till today, following cults founded by false prophets whose prophecies never came to pass.

Mankind seeks the Divine. There is always a hunger to be reunited with the Father in Heaven. But we learn in our Church that the journey to the Father is through the world's *crosses and struggles.* There are no short cuts. Each step we take, carrying our own cross, brings us closer to Jesus Who carried His Cross out of love for us, right to His death on Calvary. *How do we know the truth?* Jesus left us an earthly father - our Pope who will, like all good and holy fathers, guide us on this journey of passing earthly life to eternal life. The way is not through space ships. We must take the path left by our Lord Jesus Christ. As we were redeemed through *His* Cross, so we must pick up *our* crosses and follow Him.

This tragedy had a profound and devastating effect which reverberated throughout the world, and we must ask ourselves how this could happen. Bright sensitive people, of all ages ranging from those in their twenties to those in their seventies, chose to die in a most grotesque manner defying all human reasoning. As we are living this nightmare, grieving for those who died so horribly and for their families who will never be the same, we must try to sift through the ashes, to understand what God wants to tell us through this senseless disaster. *Take cults seriously!* Don't buy into *Your loved ones will come back.* Stop them before they leave, before they fall prey to the enemy of God who is using all sorts of twisted souls to do his dirty work. We must fight for our children. We must be *more* dedicated than those who would destroy our young. We didn't know why this book took eight years to write, but with each passing day, we can see God's plan and timetable.

* * *

In 1990, Desert Storm was raging in Kuwait. Our boys were over there defending the Kuwaitis against the Iraqis. But the strange thing was that our boys fighting in Kuwait could not have a Bible with them. To be found with any form of literature of a religious nature (outside of the Moslem Koran) meant imprisonment of our servicemen by the Kuwaitis. So much for the Kuwaitis whom we were defending.

Now, in our village in Southern California, no matter how many thousands of names we presented, petitioning our Cable Company, we could not receive EWTN. But this one day, surfing with the remote control on our television set, who should we see and hear in our living room but a white woman dressed as a Moslem, condemning the United States for cruelty and abuses being waged against *poor* Iraqi citizens. She also boasted that the Moslem world would take over the United States and the rest of the world by sheer numbers - their 10-15 children per family as opposed to our 1 1/3 per family.

If this disturbing anti-American propaganda invading our home and our peace was not enough to get our attention, where did our remote land next? There was this woman on the screen dressed in an outfit resembling that of a priest - chasuble, stole and all, and she was *channeling*; only at this time I didn't know what channeling[3] was. She sounded like a robot spitting out words with the rat-tat-tat ear-shattering cadence of an assault rifle. She stood in front of a huge picture of what looked like a giant host; to the left was a picture of someone resembling Jesus. On the altar in back of her stood a tabernacle, a statue of Our Lady of Fatima, a monstrance, a statue of Buddha and representations of other religions. She was covering all bases. I thought to myself *Who would take her seriously? Who would listen to this jibberish?*

The Church Universal and Triumphant (or CUT)

We found out that the woman on the screen was *Elizabeth Clare Prophet*, otherwise known as "Ma Guru" by her followers. She met Mark Prophet (former insurance salesman), founder of the *Church Universal and Triumphant*, when she was a student at Boston University; after the two divorced their respective spouses they married. He claimed to be a reincarnated Sir Lancelot. The Prophets eventually moved their escalating following to Colorado. There Mark Prophet died of what Elizabeth claims was a sudden heart attack. She took over the cult and moved from Colorado to

Malibu where she and her cult moved into over 250 acres (which she purchased) nestled in the breathtakingly beautiful hills overlooking the Pacific Ocean. Upon receiving what she maintained was a message from St. Germain,[4] that the end was near, she moved to Montana where she purchased 12,000 acres near Yellowstone National Park from Malcom Forbes for $7.35 million.

She claims to receive messages from Jesus, Pope John XXIII, Confucious, the Saints and all the Angels in Heaven,[5] and that she is to transmit them to the world. She also alleges she receives spiritual direction from Buddha, Shakespeare, Christopher Columbus, Merlin the magician and someone called Cosmic Master Ray-O-Light. Calling herself *Mistress of the Universe*, she claims not only that she has lived thousands of times, but that we all have. Her cult believes in *"reincarnation."*

What attracts thousands to her, thousands who give up home, family, friends and professions to become literal slaves to her[6] is her Apocalyptic prophesies about the imminent end of the world, although her prophecies have fizzled over and over again? Isn't it strange how people keep on believing after being deluded over and over again, how they keep on following those who deceive them? How do seemingly sane, often very intelligent people buy shelter space (in preparation for a nuclear war) ranging anywhere from $5000.00 to $10,000.00 with plumbing? They number over 3,000 members on the 30,000 acre ranch.

This cult is worth over *50 million dollars!* A great source of income comes from those who, upon entering, have relinquished all their worldly assets to the cult. Another means of financing the cult's huge operation is their highly lucrative propaganda machine, a printing plant which is used exclusively to promote their agenda and philosophy. They have a well-trained highly professional sales force, made up of members of the cult, which is not only used to promote their books and literature but generates huge revenues.

One of the claims against her and the cult has been, when a member becomes disenchanted and wants to leave, he/she is given one of three options: (1)to remain, (2)to leave and pay large sums of money or (3)having his/her reputation ruined by scandal. As with most cults, upon entrance, a public confession amongst the members is required, only to be used against the poor disillusioned member when he or she attempts to defect.[7]

Elizabeth Claire Prophet and her cult have purchased and own over 30, 000 acres of the most lush meadowland in Montana. The poor residents of this beautiful state are distraught over the damage that is being done from the waste that is spilling over from the Cult's compound polluting Yellowstone National Park. Although she preaches love and peace, her members are heavily armed. One of her husbands (#4) - a CUT vice president was arrested for trafficking in munitions. He pleaded guilty to using an assumed name to purchase armor-piercing ammunition and semi-automatic rifles. He served a month in jail and three months under house arrest at the compound.

Cults are dangerous! But how dangerous is dangerous? One day a young woman called our Ministry. She shared that her husband had expressed his desire to join the Catholic Church. He became attracted to the Church, through listening to her pastor each Sunday at Mass. So, the young woman began inviting the priest to dinner. Instead of bringing the young husband the beautiful and glorious Truth contained in the Church's teaching, the priest began spouting one heresy after another, including there is no Hell, Purgatory or Heaven, there is no need to go to confession, the Bible consists of stories accumulated by many to teach a particular society at a particular time in the Church's history, and on and on. The woman was so very upset! She told our girl, *"I think I'll bring him to Elizabeth Clare Prophet. She is a real Catholic."* What could have given this poor innocent soul the idea that Prophet was Catholic?

Sadly, many of her followers are Catholics! They fall prey to her books and tapes. Catholics go with *Elizabeth Clare Prophet* on pilgrimages to Fatima, only to be led to *her* and *her cult* rather than to Jesus, Mary and the Church. She masks her agenda with books and videos disguised with covers and titles pretending to be Catholic. With this clever deception she reels in uninformed, unaware, and thoroughly innocent lambs into her cult. Under the publishing name of Summit University Press (owned by the cult) she distributes in often unaware Christian bookstores, books entitled: *My Soul Doth Magnify the Lord: New Age Rosary.* Mary's words *"My Soul Doth Magnify the Lord"* and the word *"Rosary"* would lead Catholics to believe this book was truly Catholic. It is anything but Catholic!

Many Catholics, as well as Protestants, seeing titles such as these in Christian Bookstores often fail to recognize the cleverly concealed Occult underneath. As with the father of lies[8] who is not only a poor imitator of the Truth, but a deadly distorter of the Truth, this cult makes a tape on the *Rosary.* Only it is a *New Age* Rosary! The prayers of this Rosary have nothing to do with God the Father but rather to man who is god. It is filled with this and other heresies borrowed from tired old heresies, long condemned by Councils down through the history of the Church.[11] This is just another attack on God, maybe the last ditch effort to drag God's children down to hell.

Titles, such phrases as *"New Age Teachings of Mother Mary"* are again deceiving, because most Catholics do not know *New Age Teachings* endanger their immortal souls! So using Mother Mary, who is endearing to Catholics, they are leading the faithful to a road away from the Truth. Once someone buys one book, and is brainwashed by its sly ideology, they may unknowingly graduate to titles with more easily identifiable titles such as: *Climb the Highest Mountain*, *The Path of Higher Self*, *The Science of the Spoken Word*, *St. Germain on Alchemy: For the Adept in the Aquarian Age*. By this time, they have bought the lie and often, its too late.

St. Augustine said: *"Too late have I loved Thee."* For many who have been swallowed up in this quicksand of lies and treachery, it is often too late to turn back to the Truth because when and if disillusionment sets in, they are often coerced into remaining. Those of you who are still in cults, wake up; it's never too late in God's Eyes and Heart. Come Home! God the Father is waiting to greet you.

✺ ✺ ✺

1954 -The Moonies - The Unification Church

Begun in North Korea by Sun Myung Moon, Moonies started to go after young people in the west around 1959. Moon claims that the Bible is written in code and only he, through revelations received from Jesus and other spirits, can decode it.

What do they believe?

One of their rather unconventional beliefs is that there were *three* Adams. The *first* Adam is along the lines of the traditional story of Adam and Eve. Adam was supposed to marry Eve, and live the beautiful life God the Father had in store for us. However, the snake seduced Eve. She thought she could hide her guilt if she had sex with Adam. As this was without God's permission, the Moonies claim God became upset, and threw the two of them out of the Garden of Eden.

Belief #2: According to the teachings of Sun Myung Moon, the second Adam is Jesus. He taught, and they believe, that Jesus was perfect, but that He was a mere man. He was supposed to marry and have children which would constitute the perfect family. But Satan blocked the plan by having the Jews reject Jesus and crucify Him, in addition preventing His Salvific mission.

Rev. Moon's interpretation of the *third* Adam, you're really going to enjoy. According to his writings, *he* will be the new Messiah. He will marry and start the perfect family Jesus was supposed to have begun. Now get this, the third Adam will be born in Korea, somewhere between 1917 and 1930; he will have married in 1960, and live in America. Now from what we can ascertain, Moon never actually claimed to be this third Adam, but by his words, he really fit the bill. However, he died!

The Moonies till today reject the Sacraments, maintaining, along with their founder, that Jesus' mission failed. But Reverend Moon did officiate at a number of mass marriages, such as one massive ceremony where he married 1800 couples in Seoul in 1975. Although he was not particularly advocating his members marry, he liked to have these mass marriage ceremonies as it always drew reporters and cameramen, with the end result it was televised, and he received free publicity.

He was very confident that his cult would take over all Christianity. He wrote *"God is throwing Christianity away and is now establishing a new religion, and this new religion is Unification Church."* The *Unificiation Church of Sun Myung Moon* was and is a one-man show - Sun Myung Moon. It is definitely *not* a Christian organization or religion, by any stretch of the imagination.

The Moonies, under the tutelage of Sun Myung Moon expanded into various commercial properties, such as buying and operating hotels, clubs and office buildings. His earnings were tremendous, to the point the IRS came in and convicted him personally of tax evasion. His residential status was under investigation by the United States. He was finally sent back to Korea. And that is where he has been reported to have died!

In spite of prophecies unfulfilled, especially when he was supposedly the third Adam and Messiah, and he died, many of his young followers continue to follow his precepts, wandering the streets trying to enlist other young people into joining them, perpetuating the teachings of Reverend Moon. Nothing stops these young followers; some have grown older but continue to add other young members. After Moon's death, they cooled down somewhat; but they're still out there, selling goods and bringing in the money. Many of its young recruits, originally from middle-class families, end up hopelessly brainwashed.

✳ ✳ ✳

Whereas the aim of *ecumenism* has been one of love and understanding, with the hope of unity - one family of Christ with one Head and one Heart, this is not the aim of cults which instead foster hate and division, attacking the Catholic Church and all Main-Line Protestant Religions. Using their own free and fundamentalistic interpretation of Holy Scripture to foster their aggressive proselytism against all Christian Religions, adding to the Bible - revelations human and not Divine, they are responsible for the innocent, unsuspecting of their motives, falling victim to their clever sales pitch. They conveniently cut the Bible into bits and pieces to prove their philosophies; quoting Holy Scripture out of context, leaving out words changing the whole meaning of the Author, they attack that which they do not believe.

What do these cults believe? Whatever the founder of each individual cult finds it convenient to teach, to bring about his own agenda, most often with no resemblance to any of the teachings of St. Paul and the Apostles, no less Jesus Himself. Why have they been so successful in leading so many people away from the churches where they were baptized, Catholic and Protestant? We believe it is ignorance of the Truth. When we know the Faith passed down by Jesus and His Apostles under the Chair of Peter, then no one can lie, distort or manuever us away from *Home*!

These cults, with their *Do what makes you feel good philosophy*, are offering the people of God the weakest *nothing*. For it is through the Cross that we are strengthened. If Jesus had chosen the most comfortable path, if He had for one moment thought of Himself, He would not have walked to death on the Cross and we would be still condemned to death; for it was on the Cross that Jesus defeated death and by virtue of His Sacrifice we gained life eternal.

***

There are between 75,000 to 100,000 non-denominational individual congregations[9] operating independent of any guidance from a higher authority,[10] each minister preaching his own interpretation of Holy Scripture plunging God's children into division, brother against brother and sister against sister. These churches, like all feel-good religions, are escalating, climbing at such a dangerous acceleration, they will ultimately plummet and crash like runaway cars on a roller coaster out of control. Oh they will appear to be the way to happiness on earth, but we know that Jesus alone is *the Way, the Truth, and the Life*, not a way, not a truth, not a life; but *the* Way, *the* Truth, and *the* Life. When Jesus walked the earth, He chose the Cross! *His Way* was by Way of the Cross. He walked the Way of the Cross so that *we* might have *Life*, and life eternal. And as Truth, He remains with us in the Eucharist. Therefore, as we walk the earth, as our Jesus before us, we have Him with us, to help us to walk His Way to Him and the Father.

These non-denominational individual congregations may flourish for awhile, but they are like suckers that sap nutrients from a parent Tree,[13] initially draining Life from the Tree, weakening its branches - the people of God. In so doing, they will rob the Tree of the fruit, it was ordained to bear, that which God had planned to use to feed the world, and God seeing these suckers are weakening the vine (the Church), He will cause them to wither and die.

These cults will not last. They do not form *family* - an earthly family working *together*, in communion with the Heavenly Family. These splinters which splintered from the original splinters of the One True Cross do not have an earthly father to make them one, as we do in our Vicar - our Pope. They do not have a Heavenly Mother to keep the family of God together and so the splits will split, the number of cults will increase and as with little lambs who wander away from their mother, wolves will attack and devour them. To try to understand the danger and ultimate failure of these multifarious Cults with the individualistic philosophy of each denomination doing their own thing, we need look at what happens to a family when each member does whatever he/she judges will contribute to making him/her happy and comfortable; the youngest eating only ice-cream, another child staying up to the wee hours of the morning and, being too tired the next day, staying home from school. With everyone doing their own thing, there can be no unity. And without unity, there is inevitable disunity and chaos. It would be like no one obeying traffic signals or signs because someone is always changing the rules. Changing the Word of God, interpreting it to accommodate each minister's agenda, is like the disastrous effect of each newly elected President changing the Constitution of the United States to suit *his* agenda; the consequences - no one knowing what the laws are, what the truth is - everyone doing their own thing. The Constitution becomes ineffectual; the Word of God becomes fruitless.

We are living in the time of the Emperor's Clothes,[12] a time of fantasy and fallacy. The world is spinning out of control; most people are now confused and frightened. At last, they are seeking the Lord Who alone can save them. But sadly, not knowing Him and where to go, they are following wolves in sheep's clothing, illusion disguised as Truth. But you ask, *Where shall we find the Truth?* In the Church founded by Jesus Himself, the Faith that has lasted 2000 years, the Religion that has fulfilled the Old Testament, the Church built upon the foundation of the House of Israel.

Our Church preaches Unity - the Unity that Jesus spoke of when He prayed to the Father:

"I do not pray for these alone, but also for those who believe in Me through their word, that they may be one; even as You, Father, are in Me, and I in You, that they also may be in Us, so that the world may believe that You have sent Me. The glory which You have given Me I have given to them, that they may be one even as We are one, I in them and You in Me, that they may become perfectly one, so that the world may know that You have sent Me and have loved them even as You have loved Me."[15]

How can a church or denomination which breeds disunity be of the Lord? If we are not united, then are we saying that the Father did not send Jesus? Was Jesus not speaking the Mind of the Father when He said that the Father loves us even as He loves Jesus? And those who propose to be Fundamentalists - *Sola Scriptura*[14] how do they address the fact that they emanate from or have begun a sect that broke off from the first Church that Jesus founded, bringing about disunity, calling Jesus a liar when He prays for unity so *"that the world may know that You have sent Me and have loved them even as You have loved Me."*

How can someone who is not obedient to the Church, who is not in communion with the Church which Jesus is speaking of in the above Scripture, someone who is breeding discontent among the children of God, maligning the Church Jesus founded, be of God? When someone ignores or demeans the Scripture where Jesus calls Peter - Rock and tells Peter that upon this Rock He will build His Church, is he not speaking out against Jesus alive in His Word? The enemies of Christ are united! By our disunity are we not tools of the enemies of Christ? Learn and speak with love to those who have strayed. Ask them to come back Home; Jesus is waiting for them.

Footnotes

[1] Mt 24:24, Mk 13:22

[2] Col 2:8

[3] Channeling - Possession of a body and spirit by a foreign spirit - a more sophisticated version of seances and mediums. In channeling they eliminate the middle man, and the spirit who takes over a body is not usually a loved one, but some powerful diabolical spirit guide or ascended master, based on whom you ask. A key word here is possession!

[4] an occultist from the 18th century

[5] People Magazine June 4, 1990

[6] as followers who have run away from her compound have testified

[7] People Magazine June 4, 1990

[8] another name for Satan

[9] For more on this and other heresies, read *Scandal of the Cross and Its Triumphs, Heresies throughout the History of the Church*

[10] resource: *Churches offering worship without labels* - article in U.S.A. Today - January 27, 1997

[11] as in the Roman Catholic Church - our Pope, our Bishops

[12] the Church Jesus founded - the Roman Catholic Church

[13] where the Emperor was wearing no clothes, but no one had the courage to acknowledge it, until a little child said simply, *He is not wearing any clothes.*

[14] Jn 17:20-24

[15] Scripture alone

The Hindu Connection

It's very scary when you find that you have enough material on any given cult to make a whole chapter on it. We had originally written about *Transcendental Meditation* and then we decided we would write about *Hare Krishnas*. When we looked for it in one of our resource books, we found it listed under "**Hindu Communities.**" We didn't realize we had a whole community of cults from India attacking us. But we should have, when you think of *New Age* and how deeply immersed it is in Hinduism.

The Hindus began their mission to rob the United States of Jesus, over a hundred years ago. They opened an organization called *Vedanta* Society of New York in 1894, after their representative, Swami Vivekananda attended the 1893 World's Parliament of Religions in Chicago.

When you delve into their philosophy it sounds like the *one-world order* we've heard promoted so much, particularly in the last five years. The Hindus insist on *oneness* in religions, as expressed in the monistic texts of Hindu philosophy, one religion and naturally it is Hindu! There have been expressions tossed about, some in accepted religious reading, that are nothing more or less than **Hindu** terms. They have infiltrated Catholic churches schools and CCD classes, as well as those of our Protestant brothers and sisters. You need to know them. Many of these, we wrote about in our book on *heresies attacking the Church*.[1]

We speak of *impending danger*! Our children are in danger of losing their immortal souls. We must protect them. Should you approach lion cubs in the forest, you can expect to face an angry lioness ready to attack.

❊ ❊ ❊

Cults like these are extremely devious because they are so often cleverly disguised. Most deadly, are the often too subtle attacks from within, as we discovered in one of the Parishes where we would go to Eucharistic Adoration. We had just finished our *holy hour* in the Chapel when we spotted a pack of book reports, written by fifth graders, with the heading: "**Mantra**." We immediately brought it to the attention of the pastor of the Church. We told him Mantra was part of a Hindu religious ceremony. He investigated and told us the CCD children were learning to use the word Mantra as a form of prayer. The book they were using was published by a Catholic resource, bore the Imprimatur and been given the blessing of the Archdiocese.

We told him what we had found in the Dictionary:

Mantra - Hinduism - a hymn or portion of text, especially from the **Veda**, chanted or intoned as an incantation or prayer. *We looked up Veda.*

Veda - Any of four ancient, sacred books of *Hinduism*, consisting of psalms, chants, sacred formulas, etc.

Just below *Veda* was **Vedanta**, which stems from Veda

Vedanta - A Hindu system of monistic or pantheistic philosophy based on the Vedas.

Pantheism; - is a heresy which began in the garden of Eden, but which was formalized in 1705 by a former Irish Catholic John Toland.

Pantheism maintains that God is part of His creation (Immanence).

Catholics believe that God is present in His creation, but not part of it (Transcendence).

Pantheists believe that there is no personal God.

Monism Doctrine that there is only one ultimate substance or principle, whether mind (idealism), matter (materialism) or some third thing that is the basis of both.

We want you to consider that if a young person learns Mantras in CCD or Catholic grade school, and then goes on to college, where Transcendentalism is being proselytized, he/she can easily get caught up in this really dangerous cult because his thinking will be, *"Well, we learned Mantras in Catholic School and they were okay. Why not here in college?*

Another example of the deadly enemy's underhandedness: There has been an ongoing battle regarding *Christian* television. EWTN has the best Catholic and Christian programming in the world; but there are cable operators who have refused to give EWTN its own access, insisting there should only be one religious channel which would include all forms of Protestantism, Fundamentalism, Jehovah's Witnesses, Mormons, Moslems, Paganism, Occult, New Age, Satanism, various cults, sects and on and on.

They would like to limit religious broadcasting to one channel. To this end, they created VISN, which is a mixture of various types of religious programming. Catholic falls into the one category of Christian as does TBN, CBN and any other Christian broadcaster. Together, they get one spot. Then, in addition to Christian (including Catholic), you have every other cult, sect or religion airing their programs. Each gets a half hour or hour program.

What they propose is this: Let's say you're watching Bob and Penny Lord, or any one of the programs offered on EWTN; at the commercial, or program break, you go into the kitchen to get something, then come back for the continuation of our program; but without your knowledge, it is the beginning of a new program. You think you are watching a Catholic program and instead you are being led astray by any one of a number of cults (like those in this book or any one of a thousands of cults). We, as *adults*, will be hard-pressed to realize we've just gone from Catholic teaching to cult teaching. Our children don't stand a chance.

The Hindu philosophy is completely anti-Christian.

The Hindus have a center near Calcutta, India dedicated to the proselytizing of the United States. It is there that the administration and guidance of about fifteen places in the United States devoted exclusively to the cultivating and promoting of Hindu religions and philosophy in our country, is charted, and the road map leads to the obliteration of all that is Christian.

In 1925, the Self-Realization Fellowship was imported from India by Swami Yogananda, who first brought it to Boston. The cult formed a *"Church of All Religions,"* which would supposedly combine Hindu and Christian elements. This is nothing more than a bridge over which Christians can be brought into Hinduism slowly, and then just as slowly be weaned off Christianity into solely Hinduism. There have been many arms to the various Hindu ambitions in the United States. In this chapter, we will focus on two, *Transcendental Meditation* and *Hare Krishna*.

Transcendental Meditation

Memories! We remember when we first heard the term *Transcendental Meditation*. Our son Richard had begun classes at the University of California, Westwood, when he came home and announced he did not believe in God. We used all the logical reasons there was a God, trying to reach our very bright son, but to no avail. Then time went by and he hit us with a new one - *Transcendental Meditation*. I remember him telling us how he had found *peace*, that there was a garden there, where he could get in touch with God. He no longer believed in Jesus, he said. Just remembering, I could cry. We didn't know that it was not our son speaking but the drugs!

This was in the early 70's,[2] the whole world was running wild, like a runaway train, the conductor having left, the

motor running. But *The Conductor* had not left us. We
didn't know it then, but Jesus was with us.

What is Transcendental Meditation about?

Dig deep into the history of any of the *New Age* beliefs
and you will find *Hindu roots*. It is no different with
Transcendental Meditation whose Guru and founder -
Maharishi Mahesh Yogi began first receiving an education
in the *Hindu* religion. He took many of their fundamental
teachings and modified them to appeal to our Western
mentality and spirit. [The crazy thing is that the *Hindu
religion* has *failed* in India, whereas a tiny Catholic Nun,
with a band of other Catholic Nuns, combing the streets of
Calcutta, picking up the dying, cleaning them, feeding them,
and giving them a happy death, has *succeeded*; and Mother
Theresa will tell you that she and her Nuns couldn't do it
without her Lord in the Eucharist. But we, in the United
States are falling for this cleverly disguised gift from the
enemy of God - the devil.]

"There are Seven States of Consciousness

(1) *Waking consciousness:* mind and body awake and
alert.

(2) *Sleeping consciousness:* mind and body in a state of
rest, not awake and alert.

(3) *Dreaming consciousness:* mind resting (not awake
or alert); body active (dreams are activity in the brain).

(4) *Transcendental consciousness*; mind conscious
(awake and alert); in a deep state of rest.

(5) *Cosmic consciousness*

(6) *God consciousness* now this one is going to cost
hundreds of additional dollars to be able to go from the
first five steps to this sixth one.

(7) *Unity consciousness* - This is classic Hindu
philosophy! - where the devotee succumbs completely
to the object of devotion."[3]

One of the very dangerous things that we read is that one *dives* from the surface of the mind to the quiet, silent, unchanging depths of the mind and beyond. This diving disquiets my spirit. Many of these types of mind control mediums tell you to completely close your mind and think of nothing. At some of their conferences when they have been able to achieve this type of consciousness, it has often resulted in hysteria, many becoming completely disoriented, with some losing their minds altogether.

I remember this former TM instructor[4] writing that the states of *consciousness* are real and they are a highly charged, *exhilarating experience*, but the price is the problem - the loss of ones mind, of ones soul?

How did TM get started in the United States?

Maharishi began his program in the United States, calling it the *"Spiritual Regeneration Movement."* He spoke of the 5th stage of consciousness as *Christ consciousness* where he became so *enlightened*[5] he actually became Christ. He justified his wild notions, and explained away future rejections, by saying he and they (his followers), should expect persecutions[6] from those on the outside who were not enlightened enough to understand - sounds like elitism, another heresy![7]

Wanting to get inside schools, Maharishi changed his philosophy from *religion to science*, calling *TM* now *Science of Creative Intelligence.* In this way, he was able to get his demonic practices into schools, monasteries, businesses, anywhere where they were ignorant enough to accept it and through this he was able to accrue great sums of money. For make no mistake about it, with his string of Rolls Royces and Mansions, he was in it primarily for the money. Of course, the power was not bad, either!

I don't know what happened, but he changed his course again and turned to the *spiritual* attack! After all, he had been in the business of New Age and spiritualism way before today's modern gurus! He had been talking about *channeling, spirit guides*, and other *New Age* jargon in the 70s, before they even had a clue.

What do Maharishi and his followers believe?

Like most New Agers (and Hindus) they believe in: *karmas, reincarnation, samsara, nirvana, soma, astrology, the names of spirit guides, gems and crystals* to wear to get certain desired effects. They contact spirits from the other world, and as a former TM instructor wrote, these experiences though real are better not ventured into. She did not discount the eagerness to believe entering into the equation, but insisted that some of her experiences were to lead her to experiences which were not explainable. Let us stop for a moment. Do we believe that the devil exists? We had better; his greatest triumph would be for us all to believe it is a great big joke! But it isn't and he is real! Just as real as calling spirits, better left in the depths of hell.

Spirits are consciously invited, by the subject entering into the *spirit world* through *seances, rituals* and when that doesn't give the desired effect, through the use of *drugs*. The former instructor shared that once you open the door to the spirits, you have no choice over which come into your consciousness, and you have little or no control over the final results.

The former TM also said that, although no longer connected with the organization, she regularly receives their literature and invitations to seminars, like the one inviting her to attend an event being held at the *Maharishi International University* (an accredited university), called *"Yogic Flyers."* They are not referring to planes, either. She said that she has seen people in drained pools, sitting in a lotus position, rising as much as ten feet into the air.

Satan promised Jesus on the Mount of Temptations he

would give the Lord dominion over the world if He would only bow down and worship him. At what price, this phenomena, these highs? There is a strange thing about how the devil works; first he gives you the gifts easily and then you need more and more of his elixir to bring about the great high. So to get more, you have to give more and what if what you give is part of your soul, and what if you are not careful and you give until there is nothing left.

Catherine of Genoa spoke warning of the evil that can take over in our lives when she spoke of self-love - the power of the flesh over the soul:

"Catherine said that she saw a vision of self-love whose lord and master revealed himself as the devil himself. She shared that a better, more descriptive title would be self-hate. The Lord told her that because of the evil that a human brings about, when he seizes the bait of self-love on the devil's fishing pole, his soul is on its way to eternal damnation. Once a soul gives consent to this sometimes subtle scourge that permeates the world, it spreads like a rampant, highly infectious epidemic.

"The spirit displayed in self-love has, first and foremost, little or no concern as to whether it attacks its own body and soul or that of its neighbor. The soul, so absorbed with self-love, will go to any lengths to accomplish its end. When it has set its sites on a certain diabolical course, neither promises nor threats can dissuade it from wielding its lethal blows; causing enslavement and impoverishment, death of reputation through scandal, it cares not if the results are damaging to itself or others. Then finally, when there is not a glimpse of the goodness of the precious soul that God created, it cares not the cost and sounds the death knell, but not for its adversary but for itself, condemning itself

to Purgatory or even Hell.

"*Catherine further said that once a soul has allowed self-love to take over, not even the promises of wealth, position, and fulfillment of every earthly desire, can persuade it to turn around, not even the knowledge, it will lose eternal happiness and peace in Heaven. And so, deafened and blinded to the Truth, the soul condemns itself willingly and openly to Purgatory or the never-ending agony of Hell.*[8]

What is *Transcendental Meditation* all about? Is is not self-love, the *how can I have more, how can I experience more* kind of love. This is what the devil is selling in one way or the other. He is mesmerizing us, through one form of hypnosis or the other: whether with *TM* or *New Age* or yoga, or drug usage prescribed or illegal, or fast-food with its high carbohydrate content making our brains sluggish. [Looking around at people, one in every two obviously overweight, statistics stating that one third of our people are actually *obese*, if we were to be invaded tomorrow, there would not be enough interest or energy to fight.]

The insidious tentacles of this monster have left no one untouched: families from all walks of life from the poorest and least known to the wealthy and famous, no one exempt! It has entered the large corporations, our government on federal as well as state levels. Even our dear priests and religious have been deceived into giving workshops on forms of Transcendental Meditation, as part of prayer and meditation, yoga as a spiritual exercise. We must identify this enemy and warn our families and friends.

1965 - Hare Krishna - Hindu's gift to the United States

There are gifts and there are gifts. The Hare Krishnas are the reincarnation of an old Hindu sect from the Fifteenth Century, but it's only in the last thirty to thirty five years that we've been given the *gift* of this dangerous cult by our *friends*, the Maharishi from India. Actually, this one has a name which would choke a horse. He was known as his divine grace A.C. Bhakti**vedanta**[9] Swami Prabhujada from Calcutta. He introduced Hare Krishna into the United States in 1965.

We have always looked upon the followers of Krishna as strange, when we see them chanting in the streets, no matter what city it is, Madrid, Paris, Rome, New York, Los Angeles or San Francisco. They have disquieted our spirits. But these are our children; many of them mostly from middle-class America, could be the average kid next door. But these victims (and make no mistake about it they are victims) are a threat to other young impressionable people. We've never realized what a threat the Maharishis of the world are to our young people and to our country. When you look at these young men and women, behind the camouflage you can still see that they are all from the immediate vicinities where they are begging and proselytizing. In any of the multiple cities (like those mentioned above), they are all products of that city or state or country. They are not foreign imports. They are home-grown. They've been stolen from what could be the fine crop of Americana, those so needed for our own country.

Why? What is happening to our country and our children? We're tired of seeing wasted lives, the dying of our fairest children. We have had it with foreign interests swallowing up our riches and talent. Our young people are our talent; they are also our riches. We don't want to see them running around the streets, men wearing sheets or as they refer to them, *saffron robes* and sandals; their heads shaven except for a pigtail, young women dressed in sheets also called *saris*, wearing strange makeup on their faces and foreheads.

We're all familiar with their chant which makes no sense

to us: *"Hare Krishna hare Krishna - Krishna Krishna hare hare - Hare Rama hare Rama - Rama Rama hare hare."* The chant is in honor of Lord Krishna, who is supposed to be the eighth reincarnation of the Hindu god Vishna. By calling out his name in the above chant, they're supposed to receive spiritual enlightenment.

The life they have chosen is not an easy one. They get up early, about four in the morning, and begin praying and working immediately. They work, pray, clean, eat vegetarian meals and take two showers a day (We're not sure why they do that, but it's part of the regimen). They're very strict in that they don't use any drugs, alcohol, tobacco, meat, fish, eggs, coffee, tea or sex. (At least this is what is reported).

They live in community, these Hare Krishnas; they congregate in the large cities. That's where the possibility of major converts are, and where the money is. There are those who also live on a rather large farm in West Virginia. They are not a large group, although they make a large appearance because of the visibility they project at shopping centers and airports.

It's incredible to believe, but more than half their members are Christians. What is missing in Christian churches, which make these young people vulnerable and open to a very strict lifestyle to fulfill their spiritual needs? We know what's missing, Jesus it's You! While we are busy trying to create more fun and diversion, for the young rather than deepening their faith, they are looking for purpose to their lives, to be part of something great.

Our young are our diamonds, our precious jewels. We cannot lose them to Satan. We have to figure out how to reach them, before it's too late. Give them Jesus!

And to the youth of the world, this is your world, your time. Make the best of it; it goes so fast. This last week we saw so many of you fine young people at a Catholic conference; your eyes were shining like beams shooting out from a lighthouse. All I could think was if only this light can show other youth the way Home! Remember always we love you! Youth of America, we need you; we want you; our Church needs you. *But most of all Jesus loves you!*

Footnotes

[1] *Scandal of the Cross and Its Triumph, Heresies throughout the History of the Church.*

[2] We lost our boy October 23, 1971; he was 19 years old.

[3] by Maggie Moulton - Today's Destructive Cults and Movements - Fr. Lawrence Gesy O.S.V.

[4] Maggie Moulton

[5] Old heresy

[6] Like Satan, the copy-cat, this enemy of Christ was trying to justify his evil with the words of the Master.

[7] Read about this and all the heresies that have attacked the people of God in Bob and Penny's book: *Scandal of the Cross and Its Triumph, Heresies throughout the History of the Church.*

[8] Catherine of Genoa - Bob and Penny Lord's book: *Visionaries, Mystics and Stigmatists*

[9] vedanta bolded by authors to emphasize a point

"It is finished"

Praise God! With the writing of each of our books, we have had a crisis or attack of some kind. But Jesus said, *"After the baby is born, the labor pains are soon forgotten,"* so after each book was finished, we took a deep breath and went on to write the next one. It has been like this with each of the twelve books we have written. After each book was read by you, our brothers and sisters and we received your affirming comments, we realized the reason for the battle.

Is it the e*nemy* who does not want you to know the Treasures of the Church? Was that why we were attacked, as we wrote *Book I, Treasures of our Church, That which makes us Catholic?*

Did the fallen angels try to keep us from writing *Book II, Tragedy of the Reformation,* so that you would never know how our family became fragmented and why we are no longer united?

As we were writing *Book III, Cults - Battle of the Angels* the battle became so fierce, we wondered if we would survive. It was as if we had gone into the devil's workshop, uncovered his secrets, and he had to stop us at all costs, from exposing his deception.

We cannot remember any attacks being so brutal or so devastating as these. If these books are used to save one soul then it was all worth it. It seems that we leave a little piece of ourselves in every book we write. We pray that Our Lord speaks to your hearts and minds through this Trilogy.

This Trilogy has been written out of thanksgiving to Our Lord, His Mother, all the Angels and Saints who have always looked after us. And for you, our Catholic family and for our family outside the Church, it is to let you know who we are, as the Mystical Body of Christ, to welcome Home all who have been away from Mother Church and to strengthen those who are presently in her arms.

Index

Bibliography

Bartley, Peter - *Mormonism, The Prophet, the Book & the Cult* Veritas Publications Dublin - 1989

Cathechism of the Catholic Church
Libreria Editrice Vaticana - 1994

Companion to the Catechism of the Catholic Church
Ignatius Press - Oakland, CA 1994

D'Angelo Louise - *Catholic Answer to Jehovah Witnesses*
Maryheart Catholic Information - Meriden CT 1981

Gesy, Lawrence Fr. - *Today's Destructive Cults and Sects*
Giambalvo Carol, Green Daniel H, Moulton Maggie, Petrie Jane, Summers Michael, Thompson Donald *contributing authors*
Our Sunday Visitor - Huntington, IN 1993

Lord, Bob & Penny -
This Is My Body, This Is My Blood, Book I - 1986
We Came Back to Jesus - 1988
Saints and Other Powerful Women in the Church - 1989
Scandal of the Cross and Its Triumph - 1992
Martyrs, They Died for Christ 1993
Visionaries, Mystics and Stigmatists - 1995
Visions of Heaven, Hell and Purgatory - 1996
Trilogy Book I - Treasures of the Church 1997
Trilogy Book II - Tragedy of the Reformation 1997

Mitchell, William - *A Christian looks at Mormonism*
William Mitchell - 1977

New Catholic Encyclopedia - 18 Volumes
Catholic University of America - Washington, DC 1967

Newsweek Magazine - April 7, 1997

People Magazine - June 4, 1990

Reed, David A. - *Jehovah's Witnesses*
Baker Book House - Grand Rapids MI 1989

Slick, Matthew - *Basic Christian Doctrine*
www.carm.org/basicdoc.htm

Vilar, Juan Diaz SJ - *Religious Sects*
Catholic Book Publishing Co. - NY 1992

Whalen, William J - *Separated Brethren*
Our Sunday Visitor - Huntington,IN 1979